STUDENT OF THE
GUN

STUDENT OF THE
GUN

A beginner once,
a student for life.

PAUL G. MARKEL

Responder Media books may be ordered through booksellers or by contacting:

Responder Media
1663 Liberty Drive
Bloomington, IN 47403
www.respondermedia.com
1-(877) 444-0235

Because of the dynamic nature of the Internet, any web addresses or links contained in this book may have changed since publication and may no longer be valid. The views expressed in this work are solely those of the author and do not necessarily reflect the views of the publisher, and the publisher hereby disclaims any responsibility for them.

Certain stock imagery © Thinkstock.
Any people depicted in stock imagery provided by Thinkstock are models, and such images are being used for illustrative purposes only.

ISBN: 978-1-4705-0015-3 (e)
ISBN: 978-1-4705-0014-6 (sc)

Printed in the United States of America

Responder Media rev. date: 9/28/2012

CONTENTS

INTRODUCTION

Regardless of the field or endeavor; be it medicine, science, or the law, the moment a person decides that he or she is a "master," the learning ends. In the realm of firearms, far too often a gun owner decides that they "know enough" or are "good enough" and they stop learning or seeking education.

From a personal aspect I've been involved professionally with firearms in one form or another nearly my entire adult life. I've carried a gun as a U.S. Marine, police officer, and professional bodyguard. For three decades I have had the privilege to be trained by some of the best firearms instructors this nation has to offer. Over the years many of my opinions regarding training and operating firearms have changed. It's not that they were "wrong" originally, it is simply that as we gain more experience and discover better ways we strive to streamline and improve.

Consider this; open-heart surgery today is conducted differently than it was in 1985. That doesn't mean that the surgeons in 1985 were doing something wrong. Modern medicine has evolved as practitioners gain more experience and insight into how the human body functions. Also, the medical tools available today are far more advanced than they were twenty or thirty years ago.

We find ourselves in a similar situation with firearms or guns. The hardware available today is superior to any we've seen before. Also, and more importantly, the rapid ability to exchange information, particularly after-action reports, has allowed gun owners nationwide access to some to best and latest research available. The advent of inexpensive and mobile video equipment allows us to see what actually happened, not what we perceived to have happened.

For nearly two decades I have been compiling my thoughts and experiences and chronicling them in short articles and editorials. The material contained herein is a collection of many, but certainly not all, of these written works. While editing the manuscript I found that some of the references were dated and hardware that was cutting edge at the time was no longer so. Therein lays one of the greatest pitfalls of writing about gear. Almost before the ink is dry on the paper someone will come along and make an improvement or change. If you opine that a gun or gadget mention hereafter is dated, you have my apology.

The casual observer will see the term "student of the gun" and may dismiss it as material for beginners. Truthfully, being a student of the gun far surpasses the beginner or novice level. Being a student of the gun represents a life's journey toward education, enlightenment and the enjoyment of the use of firearms. The learning never ends. With that said, let's begin our journey together. PGM

CHAPTER 1

FIRST STEPS

TIPS FOR THE FIRST TIME GUN BUYER: WHAT YOU NEED TO KNOW.

Right now the "winds of change" are upon us and as I sit to pen this section thousands of Americans are heading to sporting goods and gun stores nationwide to purchase a handgun for the first time in their lives. The reasons for this are varied but the fact remains that the last two years set records as far as handgun sales are concerned.

From my own perspective I feel that every law-abiding, able-bodied United States citizen has the right and responsibility to defend themselves and their loved ones from violent attack. There is little argument that the primary tool for this task is the firearm, and the most popular of these tools is the handgun.

Purchasing a handgun for self-protection is only the very first step. Far too many people purchase a handgun and ammunition and feel like they have covered all the self-defense bases. That kind of thinking is both delusional and irresponsible.

Consider this; does purchasing a car impart upon you the ability to drive? Owning a car no more makes you a good driver than owning a pistol makes you a competent shooter. Driving a car requires education and practice. Safely and effectively operating a firearm has these same requirements.

Life is Not the Movies

First and foremost you need to forget ninety-five percent of what you have seen on T.V. and in the movies. Firearms operate and function based upon simple scientific and mechanical principles, not mythology and magic. Despite what you might have seen on the silver screen, there are no mystical bullets that will pick up a felon and throw them across the room.

You cannot miss fast enough to catch up in a gunfight and yes, it is possible, if not likely that you can and will miss from even close distances. In short, any preconceived notions you have about firearms garnered from the movies can be thrown out. This is not an absolute; the History Channel and Discovery have had several very good programs on firearms related topics. Of course the Sportsman's, Pursuit, and Outdoor Channels are good television sources for gun related information as well.

Firearms Safety

The use of any firearm is an inherently hazardous proposition. All firearms make use of impact sensitive primers, propellant powders, and projectiles of many types. Combined, these generate rapidly burning gases and high pressure.

Firearms are used thousands of times a day in the field and on the range by people with complete safety. This is only accomplished through a respect and understanding of firearms and ammunition. Education is the key to firearms safety.

Universal Safety Rules:

-*Treat* All Guns as if they are loaded all the time. A firearm can only be considered unloaded after it has been verified by two independent means. This could be two people checking the gun or one person inspecting the gun both visually and physically.

-*Never* allow the muzzle to cover anything you are not willing to destroy. Before you point a firearm at anything ask yourself, "If the gun fires will anything bleed?"

-*Keep your finger straight* and off the trigger until the sights are aligned and you've made the decision to fire. This is the number-one most broken safety rule. Remember, "Off target, off trigger." The trigger is not a finger rest.

-*Know your target*, what is around it and what is beyond it. Not every round will strike the center of your intended target, and many of those that do will pass through the target and continue to travel. Remember you own every round that exits your firearm.

Eye and Ear Protection is Mandatory

The burning propellant gases of firearms produce high pressure and noise. This noise can and will damage a person's hearing. Burning gas, ejecting brass casings, unburnt powder and fragments of projectiles all present a hazard to the eyes. Ear plugs must be securely placed into the ear canal and form a sound-proof seal in order to be effective.

Care and Handling of Firearms

Keep your guns clean and well-lubricated and in good working order. If you suspect that a firearm has a mechanical issue seek out the assistance of a qualified gunsmith or contact the manufacturer for guidance. Firearms are simply machines made by the hands of men. They are built from a combination of steel, aluminum, polymer and wood. A firearm contains springs, levers, and moving parts. Machines work most efficiently when they are clean and well-lubricated. Firearms operate under the same principle.

Start Small

For inexperienced shooters a large caliber centerfire handgun can really be a daunting item. The recoil impulse and noise can be quite shocking to a newcomer. Too often beginning shooters will focus so intently on the anticipated recoil and noise that they forget all about basic marksmanship skills.

For decades new shooters have been introduced to firearms with guns chambered in .22 LR (Long Rifle). Today is no different. For a first time gun buyer, particularly for an inexperienced shooter looking to purchase a handgun, a quality .22 LR pistol or revolver is an excellent training tool and a good one to start with. The felt recoil of the .22 LR is very light and the noise is minimal, though we still need to wear hearing protection.

Another benefit of using a .22 LR chambered pistol is ammunition cost. Even high quality ammunition such as the CCI MiniMag load is cheap compared to 9x19mm, .40S&W, or .45 ACP. For a few dollars you can shoot a hundred rounds or so and ammunition is readily available at most any sporting goods or hardware store.

Master the Basics

Regardless of a handgun's caliber or design, marksmanship fundamentals remain the same. In order to put rounds accurately on target you need to hold the front sight steady and deliberately press the trigger until the gun fires. It doesn't matter the make, model, or caliber; those two requirements remain the same.

As for stance and body position, you don't need to get fancy. We don't shoot with our feet. We shoot with our hands and eyes. Face your target with both feet pointing in the down range direction. Flex your knees a bit and lean slightly forward. Wrap your dominant shooting hand around the pistol and then your non-dominant or support hand around the first one. Press the gun straight out toward the target and you are ready to shoot.

New shooters need not worry about speed or dynamic techniques. Develop proficiency first and speed will come. Regarding speed shooting, if you cannot line up your sights and press the trigger without disturbing them, all else is just noise and wasted ammunition.

Begin your training by placing slow-fire shots into the center of the target. Place the front sight evenly in the rear sight and focus on it (front sight) as you press the trigger deliberately rearward. Resist the desire to anticipate recoil, instead focus your attention on a clear front sight.

Make each and every shot count. How far away should your target be? It should be close enough that you can reliably hit it. If it's too far you will only end up frustrating yourself. When it's time to move the target out, you'll know.

As for targets, you can purchase preprinted sheets from the store or simply shoot at paper plates. If you do use the paper plate, I like to put a piece of tape in the center as a reference point. You also can simply use a black marker.

Set goals for yourself. Determine that you will do a little bit better each time. If you like, keep track of your shots or scores and use them as a baseline for improvement.

Hand Strength

It's just a sign of the times that most folks spend more time typing on their keyboards that they do at true manual labor. This isn't necessarily good or bad. It's just a fact. It is also a fact that firearms, particularly slide action pistols, have stiff springs and controls that require some hand strength and dexterity. From a personal perspective, I deal with dozens of new shooters each month and many of them have hand strength issues.

There are a number of exercises and tools one can use to increase their hand strength. The Gripmaster Company has a several hand-strength trainers in their catalog that should be of interest to shooters. They have light, medium, and heavy duty ProHand grip strengtheners.

A couple of months ago I was working with a shooter whose frame was so slight that she simply could not work the double-action trigger of the M9 service pistol. I gave her grip trainer and had her practice over a long weekend. On the following Monday I noticed some improvement. If you are a new, or even an experienced, shooter with grip strength issues you might want to consider picking up a grip strengthening tool and keeping it right next to your keyboard.

Closing Thoughts

Should you or someone you know be one of the thousands of first-time gun buyers, do yourself or them a favor and get some serious practice time in with a .22 pistol. The time will be well spent and your overall shooting will likely improve.

CHAPTER 2

MINDSET

PROPER MINDSET: THE FIRST STEP

It's been said before and it bears repeating, all the guns, gear and gadgets in the world are useless if the bad guy catches you HUA (Head Up Ass). Many a skilled and armed gun carrier has been caught unaware and robbed or killed. The term "mindset" is bandied about and discussed much in print. How does it apply to personal defense scenarios?

Part One: Will

Mindset can actually be broken down into two main areas. The first one we'll call "Will." that is the will to use whatever tools or skills you have acquired to defend your life and that of others, even if it means deadly force.

An incident that took place in Dayton, Ohio, truly drives home this point. Two police officers respond to a domestic violence call that had devolved into an active shooter scenario. A deranged man was walking around the neighborhood firing indiscriminately at anyone in sight.

The officers exited their car, using it for cover and confronted the man. When ordered to drop his rifle, the felon ignored the command, leveled his gun at the officers and demanded they drop their weapons. One of the officers told the criminal she would talk with him. She came out from behind the car, set her gun down on the street and knelt down.

Being impressed by this reasonable gesture, the felon walked up to the officer and shot her though the neck. Seeing his partner shot snapped the other officer out of his fog and he fired on the felon. The bad guy was arrested, survived his wounds and was sentenced to prison. The officer who wanted to talk with the felon was paralyzed from the chest down and lived in a wheelchair for two years. The shooter lived in prison for many years until recently dying while incarcerated.

What we had in this case were two trained and armed good guys with the justification to immediately use deadly force against an obviously armed and dangerous felon. However, rather than do so in a swift and effective manner the good guys hesitated, and instead tried to give verbal commands and negotiate with deranged man who moments before had been shooting up the street. Being trained and armed is not always enough, you must have the will to do what is necessary.

Owning a firearm or any other defensive tool and even practicing with it at the range does not impart the ability to use it during a life or death confrontation. Mindset is ten times more difficult to teach than marksmanship. You have to ask yourself, "Could I really use this gun to defend my life or that of my family?" Do you have the will to do what needs to be done?

The "Will" component of mindset is something that can be learned. This takes place under the tutelage of professional, experienced instructors. Step one is to understand the legal justifications of use of force, both lethal and less than lethal. You must understand the elements of what constitutes a deadly threat; ability, opportunity, and intent. Finally, you must have moral clarity that any actions you take are not only justified but right in your mind/heart.

Part Two: Awareness

The next most important part of mindset is awareness or what Jeff Cooper used to refer to as "Condition Yellow." This is a situational awareness of the world around you. As we discussed at the outset, if does little good to have gone through all the steps to get trained and obtain a concealed carry permit if the first sign of trouble is a robber pointing a gun at your face.

Situational awareness is often called "checking your world." What is going on around you? Not just in front of you, but to the left and right and even behind you. In driver's education I was taught to check my rearview mirror every ten seconds or so. During defensive driver training in the Police Academy we went through a series of mirror checks; rearview, left and right, back to the road, repeat. This keeps you constantly aware of what is going on all around you. This kind of driver's awareness results in near misses instead of collisions.

When you are out and about in your home town do people you know walk up to you without you having noticed them? Or are you the guy that sees your friends and acquaintances before they see you? Make it a game. Determine never to let someone you know catch you daydreaming or unaware.

Mobile phones are huge attention vampires. It is all too easy to get sucked in to your mobile phone and end up not paying attention to what is going on around you. Go to the mall or shopping center and watch people. How many of them pass right by you with their heads down in their phone? Could you reach out and tap them on the shoulder before they noticed you?

More importantly, could you have attacked them, grabbed a purse, knocked them to the ground, smacked them over the head? That's how society's vermin operate. They simply watch for people who are completely unaware of their surroundings and pounce on them.

When I was a cop I'd interview victims of crime and they'd tell me the first indication of trouble was when a felon grabbed, hit, knocked them down, etc. They didn't see it coming. When caught complete unaware the chances of reacting fast enough to stop an assault are slim. By the time you realize an attack is taking place, it's all over and you are on your way to the hospital or morgue.

Parting Thoughts

Having a combat or fighting mindset is a choice. It takes mental discipline, something that many people in our society desperately need. Life is full of choices; you can choose to be oblivious to the world around you and hope that nothing bad will ever happen.

Conversely, you can understand and accept that bad things can and do happen to good people. You can prepare yourself mentally and be ready when trouble rears its ugly head. Seek out and secure professional instruction. Steel your mind. You can always hope for the best, but prepare for the worst.

DIVIDE AND CONQUER: SOMETIMES WE ARE OUR OWN WORST ENEMY.

Although this particular section might be "preaching to the choir," I feel that any dedicated and honest student of the gun should take a moment to remember who their friends are as well as whom their enemies are and differentiate between the two groups.

I would have thought that every American sportsman and woman would have learned a lesson from the dark days of the 1990s with the rampant gun banning and trampling on the rights of firearms owners and hunters from coast to coast. As a society we seem to have a collective short memory and that includes those of us in the shooting sports community.

As I sit to pen this editorial I have just finished reading a blog written by a noted outdoor writer. The subject of his column truly bothered me. The gentleman in question has been writing about hunting and outdoor shooting sports for quite a while and his name will be recognizable to most sportsmen. As I am more interested in conveying my thoughts than picking a fight with one man, I will leave his name out.

The topic of this writer's blog was the use of the semi-automatic rifles in varmint and predator hunting. Specifically singled out were the AR and AK families of firearms. The author went on to say how these "assault rifles" had no place in the hunting field. A couple of sentences down, he corrected himself and stated that these particular firearms were "terrorist rifles" and that all hunters should distance themselves from guns of this sort.

The man continued to say that state game officials nationwide needed to take steps to ban these guns from legitimate hunting. This particular author referred to himself as a "traditionalist" and admitted that he had only limited exposure to such firearms but nonetheless they had no place in the hunting field.

When I read this opinion it upset me for numerous reasons. First of all I happen to own some of the firearms that this man referred to as "terrorist guns" and I take offense at the insinuation that I am somehow no better than the terrorist vermin that have been killing American citizens and soldiers long before September 11, 2001.

Any thinking person, particularly one in the shooting industry, should marvel at the engineering genius that went into the development and design of the AR-15 and

AK-47 rifles. Gene Stoner and Mikhail Kalashnikov designed firearms that have withstood the test of time. I should not have to mention that the AR-15 is the father of the M16 and current M4. I would respectfully submit that our Marines and soldiers past and present never considered that the tool used to save their lives and that of their brothers was a "terrorist rifle".

Not an Isolated Incident

That particular incident soon passed, fanny-covering went on, and apologies were made, but the statements of this outdoor writer are not an anomaly or isolated incident. The fact is that I have heard similar assertions from others and it's not just about "assault rifles". Many sportsmen cloak themselves with the "traditionalist" title and go on the attack against other sportsmen who don't do it like they do.

I have heard bow hunters condemn those who would use a crossbow to hunt and deride them as cheaters or immoral for hunting with such a modern device (This despite the fact that the crossbow predates the modern compound bow by centuries). Some bow hunters have even gone so far as to endorse prohibitions against the use of crossbows.

A similar situation has gone on in the muzzle-loading community. Traditionalist black powder shooters have taken out after those who would use a modern inline muzzle-loading rifle. They somehow perceive that the guy who loads a couple of Pyrodex® pellets and a conical bullet has the advantage over the shooter using loose black powder and a round lead ball. Whichever way you slice it they each only get one shot per loading.

I've been present in a gun shop and heard someone opine, "I can see banning those kinds of guns." He pointed to a black rifle hanging on the wall. "I mean what does anyone need one of those for?" I wanted to ask if the ¾ ton pickup truck in the parking lot was his and, as I did not own one, "What did anyone need with such a big truck." But self-control got the better of me.

I am truly and deeply grateful to be a member of the shooting sports community. When I attend the SHOT Show and other such events it is like a family reunion. Our industry is populated by sincere and honest people with a genuine love for the shooting sports and our freedoms. Unfortunately, it is also true that there are some who simply are blinded by their own narrow-minded self-interest, are naïve, or are truly ignorant.

What every American sportsman or woman needs to realize that whatever your favorite vocation; bow-hunting, muzzle-loading, varmint hunting, big game, target shooting, competition, we are all on the same team. When the bow-hunter attacks the crossbow owner or the "traditionalist" shooter claims that this gun or that has "no legitimate sporting purpose" we only do damage to ourselves.

My view is simple. The more shooters, hunters, and outdoor sportsmen and women there are out there, the better it is for all of us. I don't hunt geese but I would not disparage another person's choice to do so with whatever legal firearm they choose with which to do it.

There are those in our society who believe that no citizen should own a firearm or hunt an animal, regardless of the method. To these people any gun ban is a good one. Any hunting ban is a good one. Those who oppose gun ownership and those who oppose hunting are simply two sides of the same coin.

We need to encourage, not discourage, each other. Don't disparage a new hunter who chooses to buy a crossbow or an inline muzzle-loader. All hunters, whether they use bows, shotguns, handguns, or rifles are on the same team as the competition shooters, "plinkers" and recreational gun owners. We have enough opponents out there without being our own worst enemy.

KEEP YOUR HEAD, SAVE YOUR LIFE.

During the last few years there have been several incidents where good people triumphed over bad in deadly attack scenarios. I would like to take a moment to examine two of these and considered what the good guys did right and how they survived to tell about it.

The Few, the Proud

On May 30, 2006, a robbery attempt in Atlanta was reported in newspapers nationwide. Normally a street robbery in Georgia's capital city is not the kind of news that would pique the interest of reporters outside of the Peach State. This story, however, had quite a different ending than most.

It was reported that a gentleman was walking home late at night from his job at a local restaurant when a car carrying four street thugs stopped in front of him. When the hoods jumped out of their vehicle in was immediately apparent to Thomas Autry that they meant to harm him. He could see that one was brandishing a pistol and another held a shotgun.

His first instinct was to get away. Autry, age 36, attempted to escape but the younger attackers ran him down and he was cornered. Despite the odds, Thomas Autry decided to stand and fight. He yelled for help while fishing a pocket knife out of his backpack. The four inner-city vermin attacked.

In mere moments the young toughs would realize that they had committed what Massad Ayoob has called "a critical error in the victim selection process." Thomas Autry was a United States Marine and he had both the training and the will to put up a fight.

The Devil Dog kicked the shotgun from that attacker's hands and stabbed another who jumped on his back. Soon a second criminal tasted Autry's blade and fell wounded. In a brief moment of clarity the four vermin fled back to their car. Police soon arrived on scene to find Autry with a cut on his hand, a bruise on his chest, but otherwise unharmed.

It took little time to locate the suspects at a local hospital. One of the vermin died of the knife wounds and another was in critical condition. All the surviving criminals were charged with armed robbery. The Atlanta Police believed that the four were suspects in several other previous acts of violence. Understandably,

Mr. Autry was not charged, but commended for his actions.

Lessons Learned

When he recognized the threat, four street hoods, Mr. Autry immediately attempted to withdraw to safety. Even if you are armed with a handgun, if you can move away from the threat without risking your safety you are better off doing so.

However, as we can see, you cannot always be assured of a safe withdrawal. Turning your back on an attacker is practically suicide. We withdraw when it is safe to do so or when we have no other option. The U.S. Marine called for help. Don't expect bystanders to get involved, but at least they might call the police on their mobile phones.

When push came to shove, Thomas Autry drew the only weapon he had, a pocketknife, and made the mental commitment to fight for his life. This is a huge factor. The commitment, the will, to put up a determined fight when faced with evil is the most important weapon in your arsenal. Finally, Autry fought ferociously. When the fight is joined it must be joined completely. There is no room for half measures in a life and death struggle.

A Romantic Dinner

What Ken Hammond had in mind for the evening was a romantic, early Valentine's Day dinner with his wife.

He wasn't out hunting trouble. Unfortunately, you don't have to hunt trouble for it to find you.

Hammond a police officer for the city of Ogden, Utah had chosen the Trolley Square Mall in Salt Lake City. The couple's pleasant evening was quickly spoiled when Ken recognized the sound of gunfire coming from somewhere close by.

Officer Hammond's wife was a dispatcher for a local department. Ken was armed. He told his wife to take cover and to call in the shooting while he went to investigate. Mrs. Hammond not only called the shooting in but she gave the 911 dispatcher a complete description of her husband and made sure they knew he was an armed off-duty cop.

Within moments a uniformed Salt Lake City officer arrived on scene. Recognizing Hammond from the description he received via his radio, the two lawmen joined forces and engaged the threat, Sulejmen Talovic.

Talovic had entered the mall with a handgun, shotgun, and a bag full of ammunition. His intent was not robbery, it was mass murder. Without provocation Talovic opened fired on innocent shoppers. Several were wounded or dying when the first two police officers got to him.

Officer Hammond and the uniformed SLC officer engaged the murderer with gunfire and forced him to direct his attention at them, not helpless victims. Their fire pinned Talovic down and restricted his movement. This factor allowed three other responding SLC officers to flank the domestic terrorist and kill him.

Lessons Learned

First and foremost, Officer Ken Hammond had the mental discipline to be armed off duty. It is all too easy for gun owners to fall prey to complacence or laziness. That little gremlin on your shoulder says, "You don't need to mess with carrying your gun. You're just going to the mall. What could happen?" The temptation to "leave it at home" is very real. It takes personal discipline to be armed are prepared for danger when no danger is expected.

Another major consideration is the fact that not only did Hammond's wife call in the shooting, but she made sure that responding officers would have a complete description of her armed, but off-duty husband. Too many off-duty or plain clothes officers are shot in mistaken identity tragedies. If you are an armed good guy you want the responding good guys to know about it.

If you are a legally armed citizen, keep your head and be aware that uniformed officers are likely on the way to a shooting or man with a gun call. They are going to be pumped with adrenaline and won't know you from Adam. Expect uniformed officers to arrive soon. Never point a gun in their direction and immediately comply with their instructions. Expect to be handcuffed while they sort everything out. If you were in the right it will come out in the wash.

Lastly, have the right tools to take care of the job. In the case of mall shooting, the first two officers were unable to initially physically disable the killer with rounds from the firearms. However, their shots were critical in forcing Talovic to redirect his attention from killing citizens to dealing with them. The officers cut him off and restricted his movement so that other officers could finish the job.

Closing Thoughts

In both of the highlighted situations we can see how good people that were put into bad situations and triumphed, despite the difficult circumstances. During each incident they used the tools available to save their own lives and in the second case the lives of others. Most importantly of all, they keep their heads about them and survived.

ANALYZING THE THREAT

Whether you are a police officer, security agent or just a citizen concerned with the safety of your family and yourself, you need to have a fundamental understanding of the evil creatures that may oppose you. Before you start thinking this is some type of psychological thesis, let me assure you that it's not. What we're going to look at are two broad categories of aggressor and the mindset required to defeat them.

In the security/protection field we are concerned with both assassins and saboteurs as well as those motivated by greed and criminal intent. We classify these as sophisticated and unsophisticated assailants. This has nothing to do with their social graces, or lack thereof. We are more concerned with their varying amounts of technical training and experience, as well as goal orientation.

Sophisticated Assailants

Most organized terrorists will fall into the category of sophisticated threats, as many have their own internal "Terror Schools." Street criminals are generally considered unsophisticated threats, though this does not necessarily mean they are less dangerous. Often the fact that an attacker is an amateur will cause people to be harmed or killed needlessly, due to the felon's incompetence and nervousness.

Historical examples of sophisticated versus unsophisticated assailants are the attacks on the Prime Ministers of Israel and Canada. Though completely unrelated, ironically, the assaults occurred within one day of each other.

On November 4, 1995, Israeli Prime Minister Yitzhak Rabin was assassinated while entering his waiting limousine. Rabin was shot twice at close range and was dead before he reached the hospital. The man arrested, and who confessed to the killing, Yigal Amir, was a law student who had served his mandatory two years in the Israeli Army prior to entering college.

The subsequent investigation showed that Amir was opposed to the peace process Rabin had been brokering with the Palestinians. The assassination has definitely been classified as politically motivated. Although it can be said that several security errors were made that night, let's take a look at the assailant in this situation.

Yigal Amir had at least two years of military training in the Israeli Army. This formal training puts him in the category of a sophisticated attacker. It was also discovered, through investigation, that the assassination was planned for several months prior to the assault. Detailed plans were found in Amir's home describing the plan to assassinate Rabin. In addition to classifying Amir as a sophisticated attacker, he was highly motivated. Rabin had three armed bodyguards in close proximity when Yigal attacked. Amir was tackled by members of the nearby crowd and taken alive.

Nonetheless, Amir had to understand the risk of being shot to death by security personnel and was prepared to accept that risk. Fear of death obviously did not dissuade him from running right up to Rabin and shooting him at close range (reports say less than one meter). In summary we can classify Yigal Amir as both a sophisticated and motivated attacker. The damage done by this assassin was tremendous.

Unsophisticated Assailants

In Ottawa, Canada on November 5, 1995, the home of Prime Minister Jean Chretien was broken into by a man armed with a folding knife. The wife of the Premier, Aline Chretien, spotted the intruder just outside the couple's bedroom, slammed the door in his face and locked it. Chretien awoke and his wife summoned the Royal Canadian Mounted Police (RCMP) who are responsible for the protection of Canada's top official. The RCMP security personnel responded and arrested the intruder.

In the aftermath it was discovered that the assailant, Andre Dallaire, had broken a glass door to gain entry into the official residence. Reports from the RCMP state that Dallaire was on the property for 37 to 44 minutes before he was detected and captured. The agency's own reports also stated that it took six to seven minutes for the officers to respond to the Chretien's call for help. The suspect was captured alive and taken to a mental hospital for examinations. Both the Prime Minister and his wife were shaken up, but otherwise unharmed.

In this case the intruder, Dallaire, a 34-year-old convenience store worker, spent a tremendous amount of time on target. A well trained, military unit will expend only minutes to execute a hit or raid. Banks are often robbed of thousands of dollars in mere minutes. Certainly the half-hour or more that Dallaire had on scene was enough to accomplish some type of mayhem. One wonders if Andre was not simply wandering around the grounds trying to get up the courage to attack.

At first the motive for the break-in was unsure, but after a telephone interview with Dallaire, it appeared that the foiled attack was politically motivated. Dallaire complained that Quebec, which had narrowly lost in a bid to secede from Canada, should be an independent state. Not much is known of Dallaire's background or training. The fact that he was armed with a folding knife would suggest that the breakin was not well thought-out. We should not however, disregard someone with at knife as being somehow less deadly. In the Middle East fanatics have been known to attack armed soldiers and policemen with knives, killing them before they could react.

We can safely categorize Dallaire as an unsophisticated attacker. However, the key factor in this case is his motivation. The fact that Andre Dallaire was able to enter the grounds and make it to the Prime Minister's bedroom door obviously tells of serious security problems. What he did from that point indicates his motivation. After Aline Chretien slammed the bedroom door and locked it, Dallaire made no attempt to break it down. The exact strength and structure of the door is not known.

What saved Jean Chretien and his wife from harm that night, besides luck, was a lack of motivation on the part of their would-be attacker. Andre Dallaire was not all in the game and can be classified as an unmotivated attacker. Certainly a terrorist with a specific intent and determination could have easily killed Chretien and his wife that night, and given the lapse in security, would have likely escaped as well.

Lessons Learned

In the realm of self-protection, what does this all mean? As we have demonstrated, a high profile VIP is just as likely to be attacked by a sophisticated, motivated attacker as they are to be by some kind of delusional mental case. When planning your personal defense plan, do not key in on one certain type of assailant. Do not assume that because you have an audible alarm system that someone breaking in will hear the alarm and be scared away. They may not be. What will you do then? You need to prepare for all contingencies.

I have encountered persons who feel that because they carry a gun that all their security problems are somehow solved. While discussing the merits of OC/pepper spray, I actually had one person tell me "What do I need that for? I have my gun." You must understand that not every defensive situation will justify deadly force. Pepper Spray bridges the gap between empty hands and a firearm. If some noisy drunk decides he doesn't like the way you look, are you going to draw down on him? Perhaps, but that is not necessarily the best solution. Are you going to get into a fist fight with him? That is not the best solution either. A strong verbal warning, backed up by a squirt of OC in the face will likely straighten out his bad attitude. If not, then you can resort to a higher degree of force.

When preparing your defense plan your mind should focus like a wide-angle lens, taking in the entire spectrum. To focus on only one specific threat is to set yourself up for disaster. Your mental focus should be all encompassing, taking into consideration the armed assassin, the desperate amateur, and the drunk needing a quick attitude adjustment. Prepare for the worst, hope for the best, and be ready for anything in between.

Sources: *The Windsor Star*; November 8, 1995—Associated Press; *Sarasota Herald/Tribune*; November 11, 1995

CHAPTER 3

TRAINING

TRAIN SMART:
AVOID THE MOST COMMON HANDGUN MISTAKES

It has been said that a wise man learns from his mistakes. It's also been said that the definition of insanity is doing the same thing over and over while expecting a different result. Having worked with literally thousands of students over last several years I've seen many "unique" ways to handle a firearm. I've also encountered some very common errors or mistakes that prevent shooters from reaching their full potential.

Park your Ego!

Although women can be guilty of this, males are the primary culprits. The greatest obstacle to handgun mastery for most men is their ego. For whatever reason men have an ingrained belief that the mere possession of a "Y" chromosome makes them excellent drivers, lovers, and shooters. Being honest, we know this is not the case.

If you wanted to learn how to throw an 80 mph fastball you'd seek out the instruction of a professional baseball coach, correct? Having found that coach, would you then argue with him that your dad taught you how to pitch and you don't need his help anyway?

Similarly, you decide that you want to become a competitive Judo player. After some searching you secure training from the former coach of the USA Olympic Judo Team. After the first judo lesson, would you question the instructor's methods and then tell the coach how you'd like to be trained instead?

Ladies and gentlemen, as ridiculous as the previous instances sound, that is exactly what goes on at professional shooting schools. I have a close friend who is by all accounts a world class firearms instructor. He has written books and received awards from his peers.

A few years ago this gentleman confided in me that he was taking a hiatus from teaching because he was sick of ego-driven students. My friend explained that during one class he got so fed up with an individual who kept interrupting and interjecting that he simply stopped speaking in the middle of the lesson. After a few moments of uncomfortable silence he invited the ego-driven know-it-all to the front of the group and offered to let him finish the lecture. The guy did not take the offer.

We all have varied levels of experience and backgrounds, when it comes to professional training, you should spend twice as much time listening as you do talking. If you're paying the guy to teach you, park you ego and take in all that is being taught. You'll be amazed how much you can get out of the lesson.

Getting a Grip

A solid pistol grip begins with the dominant/strong hand. Your strong hand should grip the pistol firmly with the web of your hand high on the backstrap. This offers the greatest recoil control and consistency. The trigger finger is extended along the slide until the decision to fire has been made. The strong thumb is pointed in the direction of the target.

Your support hand comes around and wraps the strong hand. Remember, the support hand "supports." The goal of your grip should be to have as much contact between your hands and the handgun frame as possible. Crossing thumbs, ducking the thumbs down, pointing both thumbs at the sky, all of these create an unnecessary gap between your hands and the pistol frame.

Keep it simple, stack your thumbs, strong thumb atop support thumb and point them both in the direction of the target. Remember, unlike a rifle where you have multiple anchor points, the only anchor points for the handgun are your left and right hands.

Keep the Grip

When it comes to shooting a handgun with dependable accuracy a reliable and consistent grip is a must. Far too many shooters alter or change their grip during the shooting process. This hinders rapid presentation of the handgun to the target and slows down projectile delivery on target.

We'll assume for the sake of this review that you will be starting with a handgun secured in a belt holster of some sort. The proper drawstroke begins with the dominant hand gripping the pistol firmly and high up on the backstrap. The trigger finger is *not* a part of the gripping process and is extended straight so that when the pistol clears the holster it will be indexed along the slide away from the trigger.

The shooting grip is achieved while the pistol is still in the holster. This is the grip you will use for the entire target engagement. Many shooters err by drawing the handgun, extending it toward the target, and then pausing to readjust or correct their grip. This is a waste of time and effort. The moment your muzzle is indexed on target you should be ready to break the shot.

Trigger Finger

If you are doing everything right, the only muscles that should be moving the moment before your shot breaks are those in your trigger finger. The hands should be rock solid while the trigger finger does the work.

Again, for consistent accuracy your finger should always make contact with the trigger in the same place both in relationship to the finger itself and the trigger. Take a moment to look down at your trigger finger. We all have a unique fingerprint. That fingerprint (the pad of the trigger finger) is the portion that should be making contact with the trigger face.

There are many different styles and trigger designs with their own idiosyncrasies. As a general rule I would suggest finding the center point of the trigger both vertically and horizontally and pressing that point with the pad of your trigger finger.

Common errors in trigger finger placement include hooking the finger all the way through so that the first knuckle joint is on the trigger or pushing on the trigger with the end/tip of the finger. Inconsistent trigger contact, where the shooter moves their finger from shot to shot, is also a frequent culprit in poor or inconsistent shot placement. Remember, we don't jerk, snap, or pull the pistol's trigger, we press it.

Breaking the Shot

When you complete the trigger press the handgun is going to move (recoil) and make a very loud noise. The ingrained human response to a loud noise is the flinch. We all do it, it's bred into us.

I've watched shooter after shooter fire their first shot with a pistol and the round will strike the center of the target. They then fire the second shot and it's wildly off the mark. What went wrong? For the first shot they were focused on the front sight and target. For the second shot they were focused on the anticipated noise and recoil.

Recoil anticipation comes in two common forms; muzzle depression and muzzle elevation. Most of those who anticipate a shot will apply added pressure to the upper portion of the frame and push/dip the front sight down just as the trigger stroke is being completed. The result is naturally a low shot.

A less common but still encountered form of anticipation is "heeling" or adding undue pressure to the pistol with the heel of the palm just prior to the shot breaking. This pressure forces the front sight up just as the trigger trips the sear. The result is a shot far over the mark.

The solution for either form of anticipation is front sight focus. This is a complete, deliberate focus on the front sight, not just visually with the eyes, but mentally as well. If you have a flinch or anticipation problem I'd recommend actually saying *front sight* in your head as you are pressing the shot. Your focus on the front sight should be so deliberate that you'll find the shot has broken before you had the opportunity to anticipate it. If you find that you are focusing so intently that the shot breaks and gives you a surprise, congratulations, you did it right.

Stance; Don't Fall Down

I was baptized a Weaver Shooter nearly three decades ago. I was taught the proper angle to hold my feet and arms, the percentage of weight that should be on the rear foot and the front. Hundreds of thousands of rounds later what stance do I now use? The "Me" stance.

No, I'm not trying to be arrogant. I've simply evolved. Rather than calculate angles and percentages, I try to hold to basic principles. Point your toes in the general direction of the target, flex your knees slightly (don't lock them), lean forward at the waist putting the shoulders slightly ahead of your belly. Relax and shoot. That's pretty much it.

Is there a need for a precise, deliberate stance? Certainly there is. If you are shooting a slow-fire, known distance course, a rigid platform with proper bone support is a key component to success.

Defensive shooting and competition shooting are different animals entirely as they are *fluid* events. By fluid I mean ever-changing. In a personal combat situation you will be moving to avoid incoming fire, to get to cover, or to reach the next form of cover. Competition shooters are constantly on the move. Even if you have a shooting stance that would make Jack Weaver tear up with pride, the moment you take a step your perfect stance is gone. Better to apply the basic principles of balance than to focus on angles and weight distribution.

Follow-through

I'll address this one last as it occurs after the shot has broken. Follow-through simply means to ride the recoil of the gun, reacquire your front sight and get back on target. Regardless of whether or not you intend to fire a successive shot, follow through.

Proper follow-though addresses both unconscious flinching and what I call "turkey neckin." We've all seen it and likely been guilty of it. Turkey necking happens when the shooter breaks the shot and immediately pops their head up to look over the gun. They want instant gratification to see where the shot impacted on the target.

Big deal you say, the bullet is already down range so who cares? Turkey neck long enough and it will become part of the shooting process. You'll start to ingrain the neck, shoulder, and arm movement into the shooting process. Before you know it you've *taught* yourself to flinch.

Parting Thoughts

Firing a handgun with consistent accuracy takes a determined physical and mental effort on your part. No one is born a good shooter. Shooting well breaks down to about ten percent physical and ninety percent mental. In today's fast food, instant-gratification, over-stimulated world, disciplining your mind can be the most difficult part of all. If you choose to seek out professional instruction, bully for you. Remember to park your ego and enter with an open mind.

GETTING READY FOR GUN CAMP

Each year thousands of citizens exercise their constitutionally guaranteed right to bear arms by taking part in training offered at any number of professional firearms schools and academies. Participating in formal training is a definite investment. Shooters are investing time and money to seek out those with the knowledge, experience and expertise to provide something they can't get at home.

Planning a trip to a shooting school is a big deal. You block out the time and cash in some vacation days. From a monetary standpoint you have to factor the price of tuition, travel, lodging and meals. Don't forget to consider the ammunition cost.

With all these things in mind you want to make sure that you are getting the most out of your experience. You want to make the most of every moment. Showing up without the proper gear, poorly made gear, and/or no foul weather clothing is a recipe for disaster.

Head to Toe

It doesn't matter how tough you perceive yourself to be, if you are cold, wet, and have sore feet your attention isn't going to be on learning. Starting from the ground up, ensure you have comfortable, well-fitting boots or shoes. Better yet, pack out two comfortable, well-made sets of footwear that you can use on the range.

All training schools that I know of operate rain or shine. Unless there is severe weather and lightning, you can expect to outside training. If your boots get soaked the first day they aren't likely to be dry by the next morning when you need them. Believe me. You don't want to start the day off putting your feet into wet boots.

Along the same line, pack quality socks. Pack one or two more pairs than you think you'll need. They weigh next to nothing but are invaluable if you need them. Ditto regarding t-shirts.

Regarding weather, take the time to research the average temperature and weather forecast for the area where you will be traveling. Think layers. Cold mornings in the high desert give way quickly to hot afternoons.

Conversely, a sunny morning in the mid-west can easily become a rainy afternoon. You'll never regret taking a quality rain jacket with an insulated liner. However, it's easy to regret forgetting to do so or going 'cheap.' A $2.00 rain poncho isn't going to cut it.

As far as normal classroom and range wear, long pants and long sleeve shirts are the way to go. There is going to be brass flying and that stuff is hot when it lands on bare skin, particularly rifle brass. Knee pads are another investment you will appreciate if your class is more dynamic than simple marksmanship training.

Read the List

I know most men are visual, hands-on learners and they don't ask for directions, but do yourself a favor, and read the recommended gear list. Most every school has a detailed, recommended gear list. They do this for a living, so take their advice. They know what you should bring.

Regarding the style of holster you need to bring, it is very important to follow the school's guidelines. Most professional shooting academies do not allow shoulder holsters and cross-draw rigs on their ranges. If the school recommends that you bring at least three magazines for your pistol, don't try to short cut them and bring one or two. There is a method to their madness. Stuff breaks, you are better off to have extra than not enough.

Regarding gear, especially magazines, take the time to mark them before you go to the school. Every GLOCK 17 or Beretta M9 magazine looks like every other one. Sharpie markers and paint pens from the craft section of

W-mart are fantastic for marking your gear. Trust me, at some point in time you'll drop, misplace or forget a piece of gear. If your name is on it, chances are good you will get it back.

It should go without saying, ensure you have the correct safety gear. Bring wrap-around shooting glasses and protective muffs. If you have the means spend the extra money for electronic hearing protection. These cut down on some of the frustration from not being able to hear the teacher and having to constantly take the muffs off to listen to instruction.

Physical Fitness

Few privately run shooting courses will rival the Marine Recon Indoctrination. Nonetheless, expect to exert some physical effort. At the very least you'll be spending a lot of time on your feet. If you have a genuine physical infirmity your instructors will work with you. However, being soft and out of shape is not a legitimate handicap.

You should have plenty of lead time before the course. If you haven't gotten any exercise lately, this might be good time to start. Remember, you are investing in yourself. You aren't doing it for the instructors or your peers. I'm not telling you to prep for a marathon, but you should be able to make it to lunch without a nap.

Attitude

I have deliberately saved this subject for last, not because it is of least importance, it's just the opposite.

Regardless of the guns and gear you are equipped with, your attitude is the most critical factor in determining how much you will get out of a training course.

While preparing this section I sent emails out to a number of the nation's top firearms trainers. I asked them, if they could give one piece of advice to shooters readying themselves for school, what would it be?

To a man they all replied that a student's attitude when they arrive was the most important factor. Gear issues and bumps and bruises can be overcome with a positive attitude.

Dave Starin, Training Administrator for Gunsite Academy responded, "Improper gear or clothing can lead to mental distraction and even breakdown. On the other side of that coin is the misconception that different gear or clothing will solve unrelated problems such as improper trigger control or sight alignment. However, these two areas are usually the easiest to remedy. ... Mental preparedness or mindset can enable students to overcome the gear, improper clothes, and physical limitations."

John Benner, owner of Tactical Defense Institute said, "Mental is the most important. We rarely have an issue, but people need to go to a class with an open mind and try their best to do as the instructor asks, obviously as long as it is safe. It is an individual's choice what methods and techniques they adopt, but when you go to someone's class you have chosen to do that for a reason. Try what they are teaching. I never want anyone to feel they can't ask WHY, although we always try to explain that ahead of time."

While speaking with *James Yeager, owner of Tactical Response*, he conveyed his thoughts on the subject. "One thing we respectfully ask all of our incoming students to do is read 'Principles of Personal Defense' by Jeff Cooper. We stress the hierarchy of Mindset, Tactics, Skill, Gear at Tactical Response and that book helps them get into the right frame of mind. I also tell them that practice and training are not interchangeable terms. Training teaches you what and how to practice. When a student leaves our school they will have the tools to return home and practice what they've been taught until the skills are ingrained."

Parting Thoughts

For those outside the of the military or law enforcement realm, planning a trip to a professional firearms academy is a bit of an adventure. You are getting out of your 'pond' and leave your personal comfort zone and that is a good thing. It's nearly impossible to grow or improve in any area of endeavor without professional guidance or at least honest peer critique.

The best firearms instructors in the nation are those that constantly travel to schools other than their own. *Retired Master Sergeant Paul Howe, who owns CSAT* a school in Texas, recently wrote, "Training, like selection, is a never ending process. We begin learning on day one of our life."

Whether you are planning a weekend or a week at a professional training course, you will be well served to take the time to prepare your mind, body, and kit bag. Never kid yourself by thinking "I'll just pick up 'x' when I get there." Referring back to my Marine Corps days, you should be ready to go as soon as your boots hit the ground.

GET IT GOING; FIXING THE MOST COMMON STOPPAGE: HANDGUNS

The loudest sound in the world is not necessarily the crushing noise of ammunition igniting in your pistol. No, the loudest sound in the world is most likely the audible "click" you hear when expecting a "bang." In a deadly force situation this is when things get really interesting, really fast.

When that blaster in your hand goes click instead of bang you have a choice. You can either fix it, get it back up and running rapidly or you can stand there staring at it like a hog looking at a wristwatch. How long do you have to clear a stoppage in a gunfight? You have the rest of your life. How long that life will be depends on your training and how quickly you act.

The Problem

From a technical standpoint, a stoppage is any unintentional interruption in a gun's cycle of operation. While the cycle of operation varies slightly from gun to gun, the number one, most common stoppage is "failure to feed, failure to fire." In many training circles this is referred to as a "Type 1 Malfunction." Although it's difficult to put a number on it, the Type 1 is generally the culprit nine times out of ten.

"Failure to feed, failure to fire" can include any number of factors. The chamber might be empty, as in you did not properly load the weapon, or the magazine has come unseated and is sticking out a fraction of an inch. In some cases there may be a problem with the magazine itself. The ammunition may have shifted or been loaded in the magazine improperly. Of course the magazine spring might be stuck, kinked or not working properly.

Second Strike Option?

Another factor in the failure to feed/fire is the ammunition itself. A round was indeed chambered but did not ignite for some reason. While this is rare, it can and does happen. Yes, the majority of ammunition that did not ignite on the first primer strike will often ignite with the second one. However, this is not a one hundred percent guarantee.

There are a number of firearms manufacturers and trainers out there that extol the virtues of the "second strike" handgun, the double-action or DAO pistols that allows you to press the trigger a second time even though the round has not ignited. On the face of it this sounds like a good idea. I myself would agree if it were not for one critical issue. You see, I rarely wear my X-Ray vision glasses when I shoot and I cannot peer though the steel of the slide and barrel to see whether or not there is a round that needs a second strike or the chamber is empty.

When I am expecting a bang and instead get a click, I don't know why that happened, just that it did. If the magazine has come unseated and a fresh round was not chambered or if I "fouled" up and didn't load the chamber then a second, third, fourth, etc. trigger press isn't going to help out much. Remember, stoppages are *unexpected* occurrences that take us by surprise.

For the sake of argument, let's say that you are sure that a round was loaded into the chamber and are hell bent on performing that second strike. During one of my recent assignments I worked with over one hundred new shooters a month and we expended thousands of rounds of ammunition. During a four week period I had students turn in rounds of ammunition that were duds, they did not go off at all.

If our students have a Type 1 they immediately clear it. If a round didn't ignite it ended up on the ground. We instructors would later inspect it, and if it only had a slight primer hit would put it back in our training box. During two instances this month even after a second primer strike the round would not ignite.

For the record, we aren't talking about someone's basement reloads, the ammunition in question was factory fresh U.S. Military handgun ammunition manufactured less than a year prior and yes, they were from different lots. Long story short, I wouldn't waste my time, and potentially my life, hammering on an empty chamber or dud round.

The Fix

For those who have double-action revolvers, the solution to the Type 1 is to pull the trigger again and advance another chamber into the firing position. There you are done. Wasn't that easy?

Now for the semi-automatic pistol crowd the steps are a bit more complex, but not exceedingly so. After all, it's not rocket-surgery. We call the fix "Tap, Rack, Reassess." Yes, it used to be "tap, rack, bang", but we were teaching our people to snap the trigger the moment they cleared the stoppage. Not a good idea for those who need to justify impact of every round fired.

Before you start working on/fixing your gun, bring it back toward your body. This is your work area and where human beings are most comfortable using their hands. The easiest way to do this is simply pull the elbow of your shooting/strong arm into your ribs. Keep the pistol held up in your chest area. This keeps your head and eyes up, versus looking at the ground.

Step 1: Tap the magazine. It may not be properly seated, make it so. Step 2: Rack the slide firmly and deliberately to the rear. Let it go, avoid the habit or temptation to ride the slide home with your hand on it. Believe me, the recoil spring knows what to do, it doesn't need your help sending the slide home. Step 3: Reassess the situation. Is the threat still present? Do you truly need to fire or continue firing? Is the target where it was two seconds ago?

Lethal force encounters are fast and furious events and they are extremely dynamic. In the second or two it took you to clear your stoppage the threat may have moved out of your line of sight. More importantly, a friendly, no-shoot person may have moved into your line of sight. Remember, if you shoot your partner or an innocent person it still counts.

Stove Pipe

The "Stove Pipe" stoppage (Type 2) is simply a spent piece of brass trapped in the feed way or ejection port preventing the slide from closing. The good news is that you clear this stoppage just like a Type 1; Tap, Rack, Reassess.

Forget about the Karate Chop or Backward Sweep methods. Why teach yourself two ways to perform one action? The problem with the aforementioned methods is that you must stop, observe the gun, identify that it is indeed a stove pipe and then fix it. In a life or death struggle that is wasted time. Tap, Rack and drive on.

Fixing the Dreaded Double-Feed

I've seen it dozens of times. A shooter's pistol stops firing; they pull the gun back toward their chest for a look and notice the slide is out of battery with brass showing. Some will smack the back of the slide with their palm, others will smack the magazine. Well-trained shooters will tap the magazine and rack the slide. When this fails to return the slide to its proper closed position, nine of ten shooters will stare quizzically at the firearm before beginning some sort of remedial action. This act normally follows a string of expletives that I cannot print here.

Those who are thoroughly trained will lock the slide to the rear, strip out the magazine in question, clear the stoppage, reinsert a fresh magazine and continue to shoot. The previous remedy is the preferred method for clearing the dreaded double-feed stoppage.

The Cause

The cycle of operation for a standard semi-automatic hand gun is as follows; firing, unlocking, extracting, ejecting, cocking, feeding, chambering and locking. Any unintentional interruption in the cycle of operation is a stoppage.

The bane of every semi-auto handgun shooter is the double-feed. Simply put, two objects are trying to occupy the same space. As we all will remember from high school physics class or from working crashes on the street, two objects cannot occupy the same space without serious complications.

Having worked with literally thousands of students I've discovered that the number one cause of the double-feed is the same as most any other malfunction: Operator Error.

Shooters cause double-feed stoppages in their pistols when they try to ride the slide forward with their hands. The preferred method to charge a semi-automatic pistol is to grasp the rear of the slide, vigorously pull it to the rear and let it go. Let the recoil spring do its job.

Another big culprit is the "press check" or, more appropriately, an incorrect press check. A correctly performed press check eases the slide back just far enough to verify that a round has indeed been chambered. Untrained folks will pull the slide back too far then release it. This causes the first round to be extracted from the chamber but not ejected. The next round in the magazine will pop up and attempt to chamber. Viola! You now have a double-feed.

Taking the human component out of the equation, the next cause is faulty, damaged, or dirty magazines. Cheaply made, after-market magazines come immediately to mind. Cartridges can become misaligned (tip up) in the magazine and cause an ammo traffic jam. Also, if a magazine has been damaged or abused the feed lips can and do spread out. This allows two cartridges to pop up into the action causing the malfunction.

Lastly, we need to consider the firearm itself. A damaged or improperly functioning extractor is the most prevalent cause here. If the extractor misses or slips off of the cartridge head you end up with a spent casing still in the chamber and a fresh round coming in behind it.

The Fix

Clearing a double-feed stoppage is a pain but can be completed in less than ten seconds if you practice and follow the proper steps. The first thing that needs to be done is to lock the slide to the rear. This takes the spring pressure off of the case and cartridge. Step number two is to remove the magazine as it is often the culprit. After the magazine is removed, vigorously rack the slide, two to three times. This is normally all that is required to clear the blockage.

After the double-feed is cleared the shooter simply inserts a fresh magazine, racks the slide and reassesses the situation to see if more shooting is necessary. Naturally, a second or spare magazine is an essential part of the solution. *Caveat: If you only have the magazine that is in the gun and you have a double-feed your life just became even more interesting. If the magazine is fouled you had better come up with a new plan quick, fast, and in a hurry. The lone magazine can be secured under your shooting arm or in a convenient pocket while you work on your gun. This obviously is a worst case scenario.

If the double-feed stoppage was not operator induced and becomes a regular problem the first place to look is the magazine. When on the training range, if a DF occurs, mark the bottom of the magazine somehow to determine if you have a trend. The good news is that faulty or damaged magazines are easily replaced, thus fixing your DF dilemma.

Finally, if you have determined that the DF issue is not shooter induced and it keeps occurring regardless of the magazine used, it is time to seek professional help. That is, seek out the assistance of a qualified gunsmith. Your extractor is likely the culprit. A good gun doctor can either confirm or deny the extractor issue and have you back on your way to a reliable handgun. *Don't carry a gun that has reliability issues. Your life should be worth more than a maybe, as in "maybe my gun will work".

Parting Shots

The double-feed malfunction is normally a rare occurrence, especially when using a high-quality firearm. If you purchase additional after-market magazines, be sure they come from a reputable manufacturer, not some nameless knock-off. Remember, you get what you pay for in this regard. Cheap magazines are cheap for a reason.

Lastly, keep in mind that semi-automatic handguns are in truth merely machines. Machines made by the hands of men. None of them are perfect and all of them can break. However, quality firearms, when kept clean and well-lubricated should serve you well.

If you have dummy rounds or "snap caps" they are fantastic training tools to aid in your practice. Take a few dummy rounds to the range and randomly load them into your magazines. It needs to be random so you aren't looking for the stoppage. After a few training sessions the "Tap, Rack, Reassess" should be second nature.

How quickly should you be able to fix your pistol? Two seconds is a good benchmark to start with. Remember, in a gunfight you have the rest of your life to clear that stoppage.

UP AND RUNNING:
CLEARING THE MOST COMMON AR RIFLE STOPPAGES.

Some folks view firearms as mystical or magical devices belching fire and smoke and roaring like a beast. The simple fact is that firearms are basically simple machines. They are built from steel, aluminum, polymer and/or wood. Guns contain pins, springs, and levers just as any other manmade machine does.

After we remove the mythological aspect from the gun we see that we have a basic machine. In the case of the semi-automatic firearm the fuel for such is the ammunition cartridge.

Every firearm has what is referred to as a "cycle of operation." For the AR-style rifle, this cycle has eight steps.

These steps are Firing, Unlocking, Extracting, Ejecting, Cocking, Feeding, Chambering, and Locking. Simply put, any unintentional interruption in the cycle of operation is a stoppage.

A stoppage is not necessarily a malfunction due to a broken weapon. Stoppages can generally be fixed quickly and the weapon put back into firing condition. When teaching stoppage clearing, I find that it is easiest to classify the most common types of stoppages as Type 1, 2, and 3.

Type 1

Just like the semi-automatic handgun, AR stoppages most often caused by operator error. You thought that you chambered a round but in fact did not. The bolt might be out of battery or the magazine may not be seated properly. Though technically possible but rare, you may have a bad piece of ammunition.

The good news is that the solution to the Type 1 Stoppage is straightforward and easy to perform. 1) Tap the magazine to ensure it is seated 2) grasp the charging handle and Rack the bolt vigorously to the rear, letting the buffer spring drive the bolt home 3) Reassess the target to see if you still need to fire.

Again, we no longer recommend "Tap, Rack, Bang," as we were teaching people to unconsciously or reflexively snap the trigger. That's not a good thing. Each and every time you press that trigger it needs to be a conscious, purposeful decision. You can't call that bullet back. You own every round you fire. Instead we will "Tap, Rack, Reassess". The good news is that this fix will clear somewhere in the neighborhood of ninety to ninety-five percent of stoppages. From a commonality of training aspect, tapping the magazine and racking the charging handle is identical to the loading process for the rifle.

Type 2

The Type 2 Stoppage is also called the "stovepipe". The irony of this is that a half-century ago when this stoppage became prevalent most people still had wood burning stoves in their homes and therefore had stovepipes sticking out of their roofs. Today an actual stovepipe is generally only found at a hunting cabin and few people have them in their homes.

Nonetheless, the term for a piece of spent brass caught in the ejection port is still a "stovepipe". In technical terms we could call this a chamber or feed-way obstruction. Regardless of what you call it, the Type 2 stoppage means a piece of fired brass has been extracted from the chamber but somehow did not clear the ejection port.

The bolt face, driven by the power of the buffer spring, has pinned that piece of brass against the ejection port wall. The rifle isn't going to go bang again until we clear this stoppage.

One solution offered by some is to take the non-firing or support hand and sweep or wipe the brass out of the ejection port. That fix does work. However, there are three problems with this method. First, in order to utilize that method you need to first visually confirm that you have a Type 2. This requires ample light. Yes, we shoot in the dark and don't always have good light.

The second issue is that we don't know for a fact whether a fresh, unfired round was chambered when the stovepipe occurred. Sweeping the offending brass away from the ejection port does not cycle the action and chamber a round.

The third issue, and biggest one in my opinion, is that the neuromuscular pathway for the brass sweep is different than the tap/rack method for Type 1. As the most common stoppage is a Type 1 and therefore requires the tap/rack, if your AR fails to fire when it should, tap/rack is the fix you should apply. If you instead pause, visually inspect the weapon and then decide to sweep the brass away with your hand, you have wasted time and effort.

To clear a Type 2 "Stovepipe" stoppage with the AR, refer to the Type 1. Tap the magazine, rack the bolt vigorously, and reassess. The only step I would add is to angle the ejection port toward the ground to let gravity help you out.

Type 3

While the failure to feed/fire and stovepipe represent the majority of stoppages encountered with the AR, the Type 3, though rare, must be addressed. The final most common stoppage is a Double-Feed also referred to as Type 3.

A double-feed occurs when two objects attempt to occupy the same space. In this case it's the rifle's chamber.

As the chamber is not designed to accept two rounds this presents a big problem.

The most common type of double-feed is the failure of a spent piece of brass to extract from the chamber and a fresh piece of ammunition is fed in behind it. This stoppage cannot be cleared by tap/rack.

If you've been training diligently you will first notice a double-feed after your rifle has failed to fire and you attempted to clear it with tap/rack/reassess. Having discovered that you indeed have a Type 3 you need to follow these steps; Lock, Rip, Rack.

The log jam in your action is being exacerbated by pressure from the buffer spring. 1) Lock the bolt to the rear. This takes the spring pressure off the stuck round. 2) Rip the magazine out. Often the magazine is a contributing factor. 3) Rack the charging handle once, twice, three times for good measure. This will clear the obstruction nine times out of ten. If it does not you may need to stick your fingers up into the magazine well and sweep the brass out.

With the chamber now cleared, insert a fresh magazine, rack the bolt and reassess to determine if you need to fire. Reading the instructions for clearing a Type 3 actually takes longer than doing it, but it's still going to take some time.

A highly trained operator can clear a Type 3 in five to ten seconds. The average person will naturally need more time. If a stoppage occurs in the middle of a fight you have two basic options: transition to a sidearm and keep fighting or seek cover and fix your rifle. The situation will dictate what's appropriate. If you have a stuck case (that is, rack the bolt won't remove it) that gun is effectively down until you can shove a cleaning rod or some other implement of destruction down the barrel to knock it out. This is great time to have another gun handy.

Parting Shots

As we mentioned at the outset of this piece, the most common cause of the stoppage is operator error. We forget to chamber a round, didn't seat the magazine all the way or take the bolt out of battery with a hastily/poorly executed chamber check.

Another big culprit, particularly regarding double-feeds is used and abused magazines. Magazines will eventually wear out, especially if they are designated as "trainers" and used by multiple shooters. After thousands of rounds, the lips of metal AR mags will begin to spread ever so slightly and cause double-feeds. At this point in American history, 30-round AR magazines are plentiful. Purchase several and rotate them regularly. If a magazine gets worn out and is causing stoppages, get rid of it. Don't be cheap.

Dirty, dry guns are also to blame a good deal of the time. Remember, a semi-automatic firearm is a simple machine. Machines run the best when they are clean and properly lubricated not dry and dirty. You wouldn't run your truck or car engine without oil, would you?

There is quite a bit of hype and rumor about the reliability of the AR rifle. Each year I train several thousand shooters using M4's and I can tell you that by and large it comes down to maintenance. Keep your rifles clean and lubricated and they will serve you well. Again, firearms are simple machines. Parts will wear out after tens of thousands of rounds. Get familiar with your rifle. Changing out springs and other moving parts is really not all that difficult if you know what you are doing.

Gear is great, but training is the key. Get out to the range and practice. Work on the Tap, Rack, Reassess drill. Set up a double-feed and run through the Lock, Rip, Rack technique. With practice you can get your rifle back up and running in seconds.

CHAPTER 4

TACTICS

CHECK YOUR SIX; AWARENESS CAN KEEP YOU SAFE.

"Check your six" or simply "Check Six" is advice often given by those with either a tactical law enforcement or military background. Simply put, "check six" reminds us to be aware of our surroundings, not just what is in front and to the sides but what is behind us as well. Trouble often comes from the rear as the bad guys try to take you by surprise.

In a recent conversation a close friend told me how the practice of checking his six saved him from trouble while out in public. As a bit of background, the man in question is a police officer with fifteen plus years of street experience. This gentleman was actually off the job and on vacation with his wife when the incident occurred.

My friend and his wife were recently enjoying a second honeymoon in Las Vegas. They were out enjoying a pleasant evening strolling along the world famous Las Vegas "Strip". He began the story by stating, "My wife and I were walking along and talking. It was dusk and I decided to take a few pictures of the Vegas lights. Basically, I was doing the 'tourist' thing."

My friend went on to explain, "I picked up this guy as he walked past us. He didn't look like a tourist. He just had a dirty, un-kept look to him. This guy wasn't looking at the bright lights or the water show going on across the street in front of the Bellagio hotel. He was watching the crowd. When this guy walked by I saw him eye my wife's purse. No, it wasn't hanging loose, it was over her shoulder. I was getting ready to take a picture when the guy went by and he didn't look at me."

Elaborating further, the off-duty cop explained that the guy started shadowing them. "I knew almost instantly that he was following us. We stopped a couple of times and looked around. When we did he would stop too and act like he was looking for something. I immediately told my wife was going on and told her to be ready."

My friend was legally armed and though he felt confident of defending himself did not want to force a confrontation on a crowded public street. "This guy could have been a Meth-head or some other kind of doper. He was thin and had dark sunken eyes. I didn't know what he might be capable of. If this guy pulled a weapon, most likely a knife, guns are too easily traded for dope. I would have had a lethal force situation on my hands and, justified or not, that's not something you want to have if you can avoid it."

The couple moved into a crowd and crossed a side street. "I was looking for some guys from Las Vegas Metro. A block later I found them. I showed them my badge and ID and told them I had made a guy who was stalking us. I gave them a description and my wife and I stepped aside. In a couple of minutes they had the shady guy stopped and frisked. He was in handcuffs quickly. We let them take it from there and enjoyed the rest of a great evening."

Lessons Learned

My friend was no sooner finished relating his experience to me than I knew it was an excellent opportunity to point out some valid personal safety pointers. Of course the primary concept is awareness, situational awareness everywhere you go. The late Jeff Cooper called it "Condition Yellow." A constant awareness of what is going on around you. This isn't some kind of weird paranoia. It simply means taking in the elements of your surroundings and looking for potential problems. This doesn't just entail possible attackers. Being run over by a careless driver can kill you just as dead as a dope fiend.

Another concept to keep in mind is being armed even when off duty or out of your normal area of operation. Too many people go on vacation and send their survival instincts on holiday as well. You don't have to be looking for trouble for trouble to find you. I have heard guys explain that they don't carry off duty or out of their jurisdiction because, "I'm not expecting trouble." That's not the point.

If you were expecting trouble out in a public setting you would be crazy to put yourself into that situation.

A third important thought to keep in mind is just because you are armed and likely justified doesn't mean you should push the confrontation. Even if you are one hundred percent in the right and defend yourself or someone else with force, you are looking at a considerable follow-up investigation by local law enforcement. You will be filling out forms and giving statement for hours if not days. Plan to be subpoenaed to court as well.

Yes, of course you should defend yourself. However, you need to be absolutely sure in your mind that it has come to that point. You set the rules and act when you are ready. In our example here, the off-duty cop had the tools to handle the situation and the reasonable fear that someone was planning to do harm to him or his wife. However, he was not yet in jeopardy. He understood this based upon his training and experience.

Every situation is going to be unique. It is only through training, backed up by experience that you will be able to make the right judgment when the situation comes. You need to give yourself "If/Then" scenarios. "If" he keeps coming after I tell him to stop, "Then" I will use pepper spray, a Taser, an impact tool, a pistol, etc.

Work with the local authorities. Although my friend had a mobile phone and could have dialed 911, he knew from experience that the Las Vegas Metro Police had bicycle patrols that were found up and down the strip. He also knew that they wore yellow polo shirts and black pants for rapid identification. When he found a pair of

Metro officers he immediately identified himself and gave a thorough description of the suspicious man's actions and appearance.

This last items dovetails into my closing comments. Not only should you let the police do their job, you need to help them do it. Be prepared to give specifics. Telling a cop that some guy was "acting weird" doesn't give them much to go on. Acting weird is not a crime and lots of people do it. On the other hand, giving officers specific behavior indicators and actions will give them something solid to work with.

Pay attention and be prepared to give a good description. Don't trust you memory if you don't have to. Write down vehicle descriptions and license plate numbers. If you can't write it down, repeat the description to yourself over and over; "white male, brown hair, blue jeans, white shoes, black t-shirt." Look for unique clues too, such as a large tattoo, facial piercings, gold tooth etc. In addition to physical description and dress my friend noticed that the man had dirty black leather shoes and the toes of these were badly scuffed up.

Closing Thoughts

There is more than one way to win a fight. Amongst your choices is avoiding the confrontation by outsmarting your adversary. Prepare yourself for trouble wherever you are. Crime doesn't take a vacation. Pay attention to your surroundings and those who are in it, and always check your six.

THE ACTIVE SHOOTER: MURDER IN PROGRESS*

*While there is a heavy use of law enforcement terms in this section, an armed citizen moving about in public is as likely to encounter and "Active Shooter" as a uniformed police officer is.

For as long as there has been organized law enforcement in the United States there have been "active shooter" scenarios, though that term has only been in vogue for a decade or so now. Historically, active shooting situations have been byproducts of other felonies, most often bank robberies. A crime that started out as a robbery, or perhaps a kidnapping, would go bad and turn into a shootout. We used to simply call these events gunfights. The normal situation has been the bad guys (crooks) shooting it out with the good guys (cops). Law enforcement and society in general have looked at this as something that happens periodically and, for lack of a better term, a part of doing business.

On April 20, 1999, in a Colorado town of less than 30,000 people, an event occurred that changed the way law enforcement would view felonious shootings from that day on. We should all know by now what happened at the Columbine High School on the day in question. What is most significant is that the accepted thought process for law enforcement at that time was the old standard, that being a "bad guys versus good guys" gunfight. The rules had changed, however, and we didn't yet realize it.

What we didn't realize until that day was that the criminals had changed the rules on us. They were not trying to shoot it out with the cops in order to make their escape. In fact evidence has shown that they had little intention of escaping. No, rather than a bad guys vs. good gunfight, we had a third element, the wholesale murder of completely innocent bystanders, people, children, whose only mistake was getting up and going to school that day.

As we have seen through meticulous post-event investigation and reconstruction, the on-scene and arriving law enforcement officers were ill prepared for what they encountered. This is not meant as a disparaging remark. For decades street officers, patrolmen and deputies, have been instructed when confronted by an armed felon with hostages to secure the perimeter and wait for SWAT. The Columbine incident began at approximately 11:20 a.m. The building was secured and the offenders confirmed dead by the SWAT team leader at approximately 3:22 p.m. The active shooter incident lasted four hours.

Outdated Thinking

The "secure and wait" thinking had been a standard template for decades. Even when SWAT arrived on scene they were held back until the Site Commander and other officers were able to evaluate the situation and decide if they could have a "peaceful solution" via the negotiator. For many years this strategy did work. A couple of bank robbers got caught in the act, they took a few hostages, and hours later the negotiator was able to convince them to surrender. The bad guys walk out to be arrested and everyone applauds.

The entire "secure and wait" scenario is built around the assumption that the bad guys A) have an monetary agenda such as theft/robbery; B) have no vested interest in killing innocent parties; and C) have a strong desire to get out alive. When the bad guy changes the rules, IE: they *don't* want money, they *do* want to kill the innocent and they are willing to *trade their lives* for a high body count, the old "secure and wait" template becomes a death sentence for anyone within range of the killer(s).

Upgraded Thinking

The term "active shooter" was put into the law enforcement vocabulary to stimulate thought. This descriptor spells it out in simple to understand terms. We aren't dealing a hostage-taker, a thief, or rapist. We are dealing with a criminal with reckless and wanton disregard for innocent life. The longer the felon remains unchecked the more harm they will do. The active shooter will not stop until forced to do so.

More recently we had a similar case at the Trolley Square Mall in Salt Lake City, Utah. One assailant armed with a shotgun and handgun entered the mall and immediately opened fired on innocent shoppers. An armed off-duty police officer moved directly toward the sound of gunfire and was quickly joined by a responding uniformed officer.

The two lawmen without hesitation engaged the killer, forcing him to respond to them and limiting his ability to move. Three additional patrolmen were soon on scene and were able to flank the killer, engaging him from an angle that favored the good guys. The killer was neutralized. The incident was over in minutes instead of hours.

The Difference

Question: What was the difference between the first situation and the second? Answer: Mindset. The officers in Utah, and many others around the United States, now understand that the rules have changed. These weren't SWAT operators; they were patrolmen, first responders and they took the fight directly to the shooter.

As an armed good guy there are a number of steps you can take to prepare yourself for the active shooter confrontation. The first and most critical step is to mentally prepare and understand the threat. The active shooter doesn't want ransom or a helicopter to fly him to Miami. The active shooter wants to kill people. He, she, or they are going to keep on killing people until you stop them. You can't dialogue with them, you can't negotiate with them. Your choice is either stop them or allow them to take innocent life. Sounds cold, but those are the rules we are playing by.

Next, you need to train to improve and/or maintain a high level of skill with arms. The chaos of the situation, the adrenaline dump, and the awkward shooting position you are likely to be in will all contribute to reducing your marksmanship ability. After mental preparation, training and practice are needed to reduce the negatives and help you succeed. The first officer with a clear shot on one of the Columbine shooters was sixty yards away. Could you put rounds into a silhouette target at that distance with your carry gun?

Finally, you need to have the appropriate hardware on your person. If all you have available is a handgun, you need to have enough ammunition for that weapon to get you through a first, second, or third wave of an attack. Remember, you may be facing more than one armed opponent. Even rounds that don't connect directly with your target can pin down and impede them. In the Utah situation the first two officers were unable to put stopping rounds into the murderer, but their rounds put pressure on him and allowed other officers to get the job done.

Special Agent Ed Mireles, survivor and hero of the FBI Miami Shootout advised his students "Don't think *if* I get into a gunfight, think *when* I get in a gunfight." Hope for the best but prepare for the worst. Remember these steps: Mindset, Training, and Hardware, and you will put yourself ahead of the game.

LIGHTING THE WAY: CONTROL YOUR ENVIRONMENT OR YOUR ENVIRONMENT WILL CONTROL YOU.

Most citizens share a common misconception about executive protection or what it takes to be a bodyguard. These folks believe that an abundance of muscle or simple girth is the prerequisite for employment. While it is important to be physically fit and healthy, somewhere in the neighborhood of 95 percent of executive protection work is the realm of the sharp mind.

True executive protection or professional security has many facets and there are innumerable techniques for providing quality service. Whether you are guarding the President of the United States, the Chairman of General Motors, or an abused woman from an violent spouse, good security all boils down to one thing; Environmental Control. Simply put, either you control your environment or the environment will control you.

My motivation for this piece was a situation that occurred not so long ago. A couple of colleagues and I went out for dinner at a bar and grill down on one of the local marinas. We arrived in the daylight but by the time we left it was very dark.

As we left the restaurant and headed down a flight of stairs I plucked a compact but powerful flashlight from my pocket and hit the stairs quickly with a flash of white light. The parking lot was illuminated only by the lights from the adjacent building. Only the dark silhouettes of the vehicles could be seen. Walking through the dark lot, I cleared my path with quick bursts of light. Finally, when I reached the car I bathed it in white light while I used my off-hand to unlock the door.

On of my friends had ridden with me and was walking along as with me. When we got in the car he jokingly asked if I had night blindness. He found it amusing that I would light my way through the lot with the flashlight. This gentleman is a former soldier and a combat veteran who understands conflict. However, in this case he just didn't get it.

I have been using a compact flashlight to "light the way" for so long I suppose that it is just an unconscious habit for me now. I assumed that any thoughtful person would understand and appreciate the reasons for it. But, you know the saying, never assume. So here I am with a portable computer in my lap ready to spell it out.

Lighting the Way

Simply put, darkness is the absence of light. Human beings gather somewhere between 85 and 90 percent of all their information with their eyes. What do your eyes require to operate? Bingo, Light! No light, no vision. No vision, no sensory input from your eyes. In complete darkness your senses default to hearing, touch, and to a lesser extent smell.

We spend somewhere in the neighborhood of half of our lives either in darkness or limited light situations. Don't forget, when you are in a building with few or no windows it doesn't matter how bright the sun is outside - you can very quickly find yourself in the dark.

How many times have you gone out for a night on the town, parked your car during daylight and then had to return to it in the darkness? How often were you surprised at how dark it actually was when you returned to your vehicle?

Getting back to our main focus of controlling your environment, just how do you control your environment, indoors or out, when there is limited available light? Quite simply, you carry the light with you in your pocket. At this point in history there are just too many high-quality compact lights for you not to have one available all the time. There really is only one reason not to have a light;

mental laziness. You are either too cheap or too lazy to get one and carry it.

Focusing on my specific situation, the dark parking lot, let's examine it more closely. The lot in question was dirt and gravel, not smooth blacktop or concrete. From a basic safety point of view of, there could easily have been holes, rocks, or other unseen tripping hazards.

Looking at the situation through the lens of security, we had a very dark public lot adjacent to an establishment that sold liquor. Around 9 p.m. that evening a uniformed police officer had entered the bar to make rounds. This was a strong indicator to me that there had been fights or some sort of trouble in the past. I was a cop too, remember, and my Chief never asked me to make rounds at a bar where no trouble had ever occurred. It was always the opposite.

On the outside chance that some creepy-crawly was waiting for a target of opportunity in the back of the dark lot, who do you think presents a better victim, the guy fumbling along in darkness or the one who is lighting up his path? Simple answer, isn't it?

Conforming can get you Killed

One of my friend's hang ups about my using a light to illuminate the way to the car was that it might draw attention from others and seem weird or "paranoid." The desire to be accepted and approved of by the crowd, even a crowd of complete strangers is a dangerous choice when it comes to your personal security.

How many people have become victims of crime because they allowed a predator to get close to them, too close? These folks didn't want to be ridiculed for being paranoid. Only after the attack came did they realize the error of their choice.

The psychological trauma that crime victims suffer is very real. Long after any physical injuries have healed, the psychological injury from being victimized remains. Given a choice between "paranoia" jokes or psychological trauma I will take the former every time. If you allow your judgment to be clouded by thoughts of conformity you are allowing your environment to control you.

Good Tools

As mentioned earlier in this piece, there are simply too many quality illumination tools available not to have one or more readily available. The criteria are simple and few. First, the light needs to be compact and light-weight enough to be carried in any mode of clothing. A heavy, bulky light might be powerful, but you will never carry it and thus not have it when you need it.

Criteria number two; the light must be bright. No, you don't need 2000 Lumens, but 100 Lumens is a good benchmark. We are not only talking about lighting up darkened areas, but lighting suspected predators. You need ample light to recognize weapons. Are those car keys in his hand or a knife, a mobile phone or a compact pistol? Remember the eyes need ample light to function properly.

The third aspect is durability or construction. If the light uses an incandescent lamp, does the flashlight have a shock isolated bezel? Will the lamp break the first time you drop it? Be assured, you will drop it at some point. LED lights can be a good choice as their battery life is much greater and the LED has no filament to break.

Along the lines of light construction, is the body sturdy, made of some type of high-grade aluminum or high impact polymer? In an emergency you may be called upon to use the light as an impact tool. If you carry a concealed handgun you need some type of less-than-lethal force option on your person as well.

Closing Thoughts

As far as product specifics, Surefire, Insight Technology, Streamlight, and BlackHawk all have powerful, compact, and durable lights that will fit the bill. Each has their own attributes, whichever you chose it's hard to go wrong.

No matter what brand or type of light you decide on, just having it with you and using it is what's important. When it comes to your own safety and security as well as that of those you love, the choice is up to you. You can either control your environment or let your environment control you. It really is no more complicated than that.

PERSONAL DEFENSE: STOP A HOME INVASION

When we were kids we imagined a burglar like those portrayed on cartoons or in old black and white movies.

Donning a black mask or wool cap, the burglar would skulk around looking for a way to sneak in and out of your home or business without being detected. As we grew older we may have dismissed the cartoon image but we still thought of a burglar as a stealthy criminal that would come and go "like a thief in the night."

There are two kinds of people who know the previous image to be complete fantasy; cops and victims of crime. Burglars are rarely stealthy; their tool of choice is a pry bar to force a door or some type of bludgeon to smash a window. Rare indeed is the thief who will "pick" a lock. Ninety-nine point nine percent will just boot the door or smash a window.

Home Invasion

While most people fear burglary while they are away from their homes an even more sinister trend with a distinct name has become the new crime of choice. *Home invasions*, where criminals force entry while the house is occupied, are becoming the rule rather than the exception.

Two, three, and sometimes four criminals will break into a home, heedless of it being occupied or not, to rob and terrorize the people inside. Home invaders are vicious, violent characters that have committed horrible atrocities against families including rape, brutal beatings, and murder. The liberal "give them what they want and they'll leave" advice has seen innumerable citizens raped and murdered by home invaders.

The Four D's

Long ago I was taught the 4 D's of home security Deter, Detect, Delay, and Defend. We are going to touch on each one of these individually in the piece.

Deter

Deter means simply this, be an unappealing target. As ruthless as modern criminals are they are also lazy and cowardly vermin. If the effort or danger appears to outweigh the reward they will generally move on to an easier target.

Let's start with the simple stuff: lighting. Is the exterior of your home well-lit and do you have motion activated lights? If not, why not? A dark, heavily shadowed home is an attractive target. After all, the bad guy doesn't want the local cop on patrol to see him sneaking up on your house or loading your stuff into his truck.

Also, if the outside of your house is well lit the bad guy doesn't know whether or not you can see him approaching. That is one more risk they will have to take.

Detect

Alarms and the signs that go with them are used as deterrents but are not an absolute defense. The alarm system provides you with detection of an intruder. However, keep in mind that when an alarm sounds the first thing the security company does is try to call the home to verify that it is not a false alarm. Only after they have received no response from the home owner do they contact the police.

Once informed the police response could be five, ten, fifteen minutes or more depending on where you are located and whether an officer(s) is (are) available. Could you fight off three armed robbers for ten minutes?

Along the line of detect and deter, don't disregard a four-legged, free roaming intruder detection system. A good dog can go a long way toward deterring bad guys and warning you when they approach.

Delay

The Delay phase can be best summed up as "hardening the target". Short of solid steel doors and barred windows, few domestic structures can keep out a determined intruder. The question is; how long can you delay them? Remember, home invaders don't care if you are there to witness their actions. If they are determined to come in, make them work for it.

The first and simplest way is to keep your doors locked, even when you are at home. Don't unlock and open door for strangers. The old "I need to use a phone" excuse is a ruse to get you to let them in. This isn't 1955. Twelve year olds have mobile phones today. Don't do it! Tell the person through a locked door that you will call the police for assistance. If they truly have a roadside emergency they will want the police to help them out.

No home owner is going to sit around their house waiting and watching for an intruder, you need some kind of warning or reaction time. If an intruder decides to force entry they shouldn't be able to do it quietly. A thirty second delay is a long time when it comes to reaction time. A minute or two would be better.

Do your doors have solid, hardwood or metal frames? Do your dead-bolts sink an inch or more into the frame? How about your windows? Are ground level windows single-sheet glass or are they much tougher plexi-glass?

How tough is it to get into your house? Have you ever locked your keys in the house and then "broken in" to it yourself? How long did it take you? A bad guy will go the same route.

Defend

The last resort, after all other means have failed to keep an intruder out, is to defend your family and home with violence of force. Yes, I said *violence of force.* Now is not the time to be squeamish. The felons that smash in your door are not going to be timid. Are you willing to allow them to commit horrors and atrocities on your family?

We've all known the guy, or gal, that kept a Louisville Slugger or Nine Iron by the front door "just in case." That's all well and good if your intruder is alone, does not have a gun, and is about the same size and strength as you. This is the real world. Your attackers will be younger, stronger, armed and accompanied by friends.

Here is the plain, honest truth. The best defense against an active home invasion is violence of force applied with a firearm. Which firearm is best for home defense? The answer is that it depends. Handgun versus Long gun is an ongoing debate.

Pro-handgun people point out the convenience and the fact that you can do things with your other hand; turn on lights, open doors, hold a telephone etc. All of these are true. A handgun is convenient, can be readily concealed from view and does allow you a free hand. However, we need to remember the intended purpose of the gun; to stop felonious attackers.

A friend of mine who runs a firearms training academy has stated that "a handgun is simply a rifle waiting to grow up." A bit of an over simplification perhaps, but the fact remains that no handgun can generate the energy and effect that a centerfire rifle or defensive shotgun can produce.

Others have offered that we use a handgun to fight our way to the long gun. If you have a safe room or hold out room in your house it should most definitely contain a long gun of some kind. Nothing says *"Get out of my home!"* quite like a 12 gauge shotgun or centerfire rifle.

Keep in mind that you will likely be dealing with multiple felons. A single shot or even double-barreled shotgun would not seem as appropriate as higher capacity model. However, if you are intimately familiar and comfortable with the twin-barreled scattergun, that might be the best choice for you. During a hyper-violent criminal action both the intruders and home owner will likely be moving. Some of your shots may miss the mark. There really is no such thing as too much ammunition.

Parting Shots

Keep in mind that you very well may be compelled to use deadly force. Long before you have to defend your life you must make the mental commitment to do whatever is necessary to save yours and your family's lives. Don't delude yourself by thinking you can bluff a felon with a gun. You can't. If you don't believe you could press the trigger on a potential rapist or murderer, don't buy a gun.

For those who choose to keep one or more firearms for personal protection, get to the range and practice. Every responsible adult in your home should be thoroughly trained in the use of arms.

The middle of a violent attack is not the time to try and figure out how the safety works or wish you'd spent more time practicing. Hope for the best, prepare for the worst.

SAFE ON THE ROAD?
HOW TO DEAL WITH THE POTENTIAL HAZARDS OF TRAVEL

Two rough looking characters loaded up the car trunk with stolen goods, slammed the lid, and climbed in. Behind the wheel was the girlfriend of one of the robbers. The two men were obviously nervous and agitated and they told her not to drive them home, but to a local hotel.

After the girlfriend checked them in, they hauled the cash and coin they had stolen into the hotel room to be counted. It was at that time that they related the full story of what had happened in the house.

Though initially planned as a burglary of the unoccupied dwelling, the felons found a husband, wife and their teenage son at home. The three victims were herded into the basement and executed with bullets to the head so they could not later identify the robbers.

This story is true and played out in the sister communities of Wheeling, West Virginia and St. Clairesville, Ohio. Wheeling and St. Clairesville are separated by the Ohio River. A while back I was on vacation with my wife in Wheeling and the front-page newspaper headlines were filled with details of the trial of the two men and one woman (as an accomplice and co-conspirator) for capital murder.

What struck me as I read the story was not only the vicious nature of the crime, but that fact that the killers had murdered three people and then checked into a hotel not one mile from the one my wife and I were staying in. The hotel in question was not a low class, rent by the hour dump, but a big name chain found all over the United States. Mentioning the hotel name here would serve no purpose other than to stigmatize them. However, suffice it to say that you would recognize the name.

The Illusion of Safety

Most of us like to travel and when we do we give the hotel a cursory look over. If it looks clean and well lit we assume that it is safe enough. Few of us would deliberately stay in a hotel or motel where we felt unsafe, at least not for more than one night. The appearance of safety is not necessarily a guarantee of it.

The fact is that the previously mentioned murderers spent a number of days and nights right next to rooms occupied by John Q. Citizen, his wife and lovely little children. St. Clairesville, Ohio is not known as a high crime area like Detroit, Newark or Philadelphia. It is a small to medium sized mid-western town much like any other you might enjoy visiting.

While you may think this was an isolated incident, recently it was reinforced to me yet again that the evil as well as the good frequent hotels and motels. I was reminded of this fact during a meeting with our local drug enforcement task force. During the briefing the subject was brought up that several hotels in our area were being regularly used by drug dealers to pedal their wares.

Although I was not surprised, I was disappointed to learn that a brand new, high-end hotel with a most reputable name had already been used by low-life dopers to deal their poison. To that hotel's credit, the management immediately worked with law enforcement to stem the use of their establishment by the criminal element. Again, this area is not a known for crime but for Amish country tourism.

Sadly, you cannot always count on the hotel staff being so principled. The truth is that far too many hotel staff members are willing to look the other way so as not to make trouble or get involved.

A few years ago I was away from home on an executive protection assignment and was staying at a reputable chain hotel. One evening when I returned to the hotel I smelled the distinct odor of marijuana in the hall. It was not hard to figure out what room it was coming from. When I mentioned this to the night shift manager she seemed annoyed with me for bringing it up. She then made a comment about "pot" not being a big deal.

I realized that I was wasting my breath and made a couple of calls myself. The subsequent police raid on the room netted not only a good amount of marijuana, but cocaine, as well as three men who were dealing it.

Drug dealers always have weapons. They keep them to protect their large amounts of cash and dope. Much drug dealing is done by organized criminal elements or street gangs. These elements often rob and kill each other in disputes over territory.

What to Look For

Although you have no control over who comes and goes around you while you are traveling, there are some good indicators that a particular hotel/motel has more than its fair share of illicit activity.

Before you commit to a hotel/motel, ask to see a room. Check the door jam on the sample room and those adjacent to it. Are any of the door jams scarred, dented, or showing signs of forced entry? Pull on the door and shake it while it is closed. Is the door loose? Does the doorknob jiggle? Is there play between the door lock and plate? Any of these items indicate a weak door structure and the possibility that the door has been previously kicked in and put back together.

Is there a solid dead bolt on the inside of the door? A good hotel room door should have a knob lock, a dead bolt and a chain / straight bar lock. Does the room have a peephole? Believe it or not, there are still motels out there without them.

If you are staying in a motel with a window adjacent to the door check the window for sturdiness. Is there any up or down play in the window track that would allow someone to easily/quietly pry it out of the frame? The same applies to first floor outside windows in hotels.

Other basic safety checks include lighting. Are the hallways well lit? Do they have emergency lights at both ends and in the middle if the hallway is particularly long? Are the stairways well lit and free of clutter and trash?

Obviously items such as bulletproof glass are big indicators. If you stop at a hotel and the clerk is behind a thick glass barrier this is not a good sign. Is the parking lot well lit at night? Can you move from your car to the hotel without having to pass through shadows? Are there large hedges, objects or barriers near the side or back entrances that could readily hide an attacker?

Does the hotel/motel have a bar or nightclub that caters to the public as well as the hotel guests? You can be assured that nightclub patrons will be drinking heavily and more likely than not a fair amount of illegal drugs will be present in and around the club.

Most dance clubs experience fights nightly, whether in the club, in the parking lot, or both. While you might not plan on going to the club or hanging around that area, you may well have to use the same parking lot and the same entrance as the club. There are certainly more items I could mention but these should give you something to consider.

Prudent Steps

Am I discouraging you from traveling? No, far from it. Your next trip will most likely be an uneventful one as far as crime is concerned. However, do not delude yourself into thinking that violent criminals could not be staying in the room across the hall or right next door.

While many socialist countries forbid their citizens any type of defense tool, in the United States you still have the freedom to possess instruments for your own self-preservation. If you are fortunate enough to live in a "Shall Issue" Concealed Carry state you will likely have reciprocity with a number of other states. Check with your Attorney General's office website for a list of other states that honor your permit.

Even if you do not have a CCW permit, your hotel room is your de facto "castle" while on the road. Except in certain jurisdictions where handgun ownership is restricted, you should be on solid legal ground possessing a firearm in your room. If you are not sure, you may want to check with your family attorney.

If you are a sworn peace officer in the United States and carry a firearm as a part of your job, there is no excuse not to be so armed while traveling. H.R. 218, the Law Enforcement Officers Safety Act, has affirmed your right to carry a firearm for self-protection even while traveling and not on duty.

At the very minimum you should possess a sturdy, powerful flashlight to not only identify potential evildoers, but to aid in your egress when the power goes out or in case of a fire. That sturdy light can also help to "drive home" the point should an attacker attempt to lay hands on you.

Other self-defense tools such as pepper spray and the Taser are better than nothing if you are prohibited from possessing a firearm. Do not discount the potential power of a good defensive knife either. In the extreme close quarters of an urban environment a sharp and sturdy blade can be a most potent defensive weapon. An attacker who closes to striking distance is open to most all knife defenses.

In Summary

Forewarned is forearmed. Unless you travel to particularly crime-ridden areas, you will likely have a pleasant and safe trip. However, do not deceive yourself with the "it won't happen to me" attitude. Many criminals specifically target tourists assuming that they have a large amount of cash and are out of their element making them easy marks.

The fact that you have this book in your hand tells me that you are most likely a prudent person. Be aware of the potential risks and constantly aware of your surroundings. Fate favors the prepared. Stay safe.

CHAPTER 5

CONCEALED CARRY

CONCEALED CARRY: MYTHS AND MISUNDERSTANDINGS

It's been said that all the best stories begin with either "Once upon a time" or "No S***, there I was." There are other tales that begin with "I was talking my buddy and he said…" Over the years I suppose I've developed a cringe reflex from all the times I've heard someone begin a conversation with such verbiage.

If the subject is steak or venison recipes or the best way to get red wine stains out of your dress shirt, opinions vary and it's not that big a deal if the advice doesn't pan out. However, and this is a big however, when we are talking about the most important activity you can undertake; protecting your life and the lives of your family, bad advice has serious potential consequences.

Myths and Misunderstandings

In the United States today there is little doubt that the issue of concealed carry is one of the hottest topics going, at least for gun owners. The sales figures for compact, concealable handguns bear out this argument. At last count there was grand total of one state in the Union that had absolutely no provision to allow its citizens to carry a concealed handgun. Considering the rest of the 49 states, the vast majority have "Shall Issue" laws on the books.

"Shall Issue" laws essentially mean that as long as the applicant has met the requirements set forth in the law and they are not disqualified for a specific reason, the state Shall Issue said permit/license within the proscribed time. In a "Discretionary Issue" state a single bureaucrat has the ability to deny the applicants permit based on the personal belief that the applicant doesn't have the "need."

Obtaining a lawful permit or permission to carry a concealed handgun is only one part of the overall equation. I've encountered literally dozens of citizens who obtained a permit but don't carry because they do not feel comfortable or capable of actually using a gun for personal protection. The reasons are varied, but they generally boil down to a lack of training and/or misunderstanding what it means to be an armed citizen.

Only When I'll Need It

I am certain that my face shows the distaste and distress I feel when I hear someone say that they have a CCW Permit but they "…only carry it when I think I might need it." My patent answer to that statement is, "If you think you are going to need a gun don't go there." Or more aptly, "If you know you need a gun you should take a rifle or a shotgun not a concealed handgun." If I knew I was going to a fight I'd prefer to take the U.S.S. Missouri, but battleships are tough to conceal.

Carrying only once in a while, when you think you might need it, is akin to purchasing car insurance that only covers you on Friday nights from 6 p.m. to 2 a.m. and every other Saturday. Certainly you wouldn't buy an insurance policy that only covered you on random dates or occasions. That wouldn't make sense. Do you only put batteries in your smoke detectors on the weekends or are they ready to go every day?

The "Only when I might need it" statement is dangerous for several reasons. First of all, you end up talking yourself out of carrying because you don't *plan* to use it. Responsible citizens never go out looking for trouble. Trouble comes to them unexpectedly. Folks, if you are *planning* to use your concealed handgun from a legal standpoint that constitutes "premeditation". Premeditation is one of the elements of a crime.

If I may play the devil's advocate for a moment, if you go about in public (posting comments on gun forums is *in public*) making statements such as "I only carry when I think I might need it," you could be accused of premeditating the use of the gun. The prosecuting attorney may attempt to make the case that you, having previously stated that you only carry when you "need it," did in fact go out looking for trouble on the day in question. They will try to convince the judge and jury that rather than avoid trouble you instead went looking for it. Given our litigious society and the anti-gun politics of many prosecutors, this is not too much of a stretch.

When you obtain a carry permit you are essentially securing Life Assurance (Life Insurance only kicks in after you are room temperature). When you've decided to arm yourself against unknown, unanticipated threats you need to do it as often as humanly possible.

Half-Loaded, Just for Safety

In an effort to seem 'reasonable' or 'extra safe' permit holders will carry their semi-automatic pistols with a loaded magazine in place but deliberately keep the chamber empty. Not on the nightstand mind you, but in their holsters on their persons. I've also encountered double-action revolver owners who will deliberately pre-stage an empty chamber so that the first hammer strike falls on nothing.

The first reason for this thinking is typically little or no training and a bit of insecurity over carrying a "loaded gun." In an effort to be "extra safe" by keeping the chamber empty the gun owner is assuming that they will always have the time and ability to draw their pistol and charge a round before they need to fire.

In both the pistol and revolver scenarios the shooter is purposely reducing their round count and increasing the amount of time it will take to get the gun in the fight. Should you be attacked with deadly force time is not likely something you will have on your side and you may need every round you have. Remember deadly attacks come as a surprise, not a planned event.

One of the most dangerous aspects of half-loading your handguns, particularly pistols, is that you wind up playing the "Is my gun loaded or not?" game. You think a round is chambered when in fact it is not, or vice versa. Also, half-loading handguns leads to the *It's alright, the chamber is empty* type of thinking. I once had a pistol fired into the ground not two feet from me because the person in question thought the chamber was empty and therefore it was be alright to press the trigger.

Loaded guns are safe guns because people treat them with respect. Your friends and family members will never point a gun in your direction and say "It's okay, the gun's loaded." Unfortunately, I heard "It's okay the chamber's empty" far too many times.

A .22 Pistol is the best thing for a Woman

While .22 Long Rifle handguns as fantastic training tools and an excellent way to learn the basics of marksmanship, they are not the best fight stoppers in the world. It is true that, as my friend Walt Rauch once advised, "No one wants to leak, not even bad guys." Regardless, there is no reason that a healthy adult woman cannot carry and employ a centerfire handgun.

Not so long ago a woman told me that when the subject of a defensive handgun came up one of her male co-workers told her to buy a .22 and load it with "dumb-dumb" rounds. Yes, that was the exact term he used. Dumb-dumb rounds aside, the purpose of defensive shooting is to force the attacker to *stop*, not to bleed to death twenty minutes later.

A centerfire pistol or revolver with a bore dimension of .35 inch and up is a good place to start. Concealable handguns from .380ACP up to .45ACP abound and are readily available. The recoil impulse from the .45ACP is generally less severe than a .40S&W from the same sized platform. I've encountered numerous women who could run an M1911-style pistol like no one's business. The question was not the sex of the shooter or their size but the level of training and experience.

Carry Gun versus Range Gun

Another common trend I've run into is the carry gun versus the practice or range gun. Folks will go out and purchase the latest, greatest compact or sub-compact pistol. They'll boast to their buddies about how easy it is to carry and conceal. They can carry it all day and forget it's in their pocket. That's covers step one; be armed.

When it comes time to hit the range these very same guys pull out a pistol with a five or six inch barrel, target sights, and meticulously tuned trigger. From ten yards they set about punching tight groups in paper targets and call it training.

Don't get me wrong, shooting should be an enjoyable recreation. It can be a great way to spend an afternoon. However, if you bought a compact .380ACP pistol for "personal protection" and still haven't gotten through your first box of fifty rounds you are kidding yourself if you think you are ready to save your life with it.

By their very design, compact, lightweight pistols and revolvers are easy to carry and difficult to shoot well. These guns demand that you train, then practice with them. You might be able to plink a soda can a twenty yards with a Ruger MkIII pistol but that's not likely the gun you'll have on your person when the bad guy shows up unexpected. Can you hit a soda can at ten feet with your little pocket pistol?

This is an easy trap to fall into. Your shot groups don't look as good with the pocket gun as they do with your larger target pistol. Park your ego and practice with that little gun. You might be glad one day that you did.

Great Uncle Joe's Pistol

Many people who decide to carry a gun for personal protection are not "gun people." They don't subscribe to any gun magazines and don't know or care about the history or nomenclature of firearms. All they know is that they need to have a gun for personal protection. I've run into this many times during Concealed Carry training courses. I've spoken to several trainers across the nation and this seems to be a trend.

Students, many who are women, will arrive at the class with gun handed down to them by Great Uncle Joe or their Grandpa Jim. Some have never put a single shot through the gun but they load them up with the ammo Uncle Joe gave them and keep them on the nightstand, in car, or their purses.

The problem with this is far too many of these family heirlooms are in such poor condition that they cannot be relied upon to fire two rounds in succession. During one course I had a lady show up with a double-action revolver given to her by Grandpa. The timing of the cylinder was so out of whack that it took her three to four trigger pulls to get a cartridge to fire.

During the next course a shooter arrived with a compact .22 LR semi-automatic pistol passed down by a relative. This person had it for two years and had never fired a round through it. When it came time for the live-fire portion we discovered that it was essentially a single shot pistol. The little gun malfunctioned after the first shot and would not cycle and feed from the magazine. Again, this citizen had been keeping that gun loaded up "just in case". The good news is that when these folks show up for a training class it becomes immediately, if not painfully, obvious that they have been getting by on luck for a long time.

Training and Practice

Unfortunately too many folks feel that *owning* a gun takes care of the personal protection issue. Jeff Cooper once said that owning a gun doesn't make you any more an armed citizen than owning a guitar makes you a musician.

It really is not possible to train yourself. You can practice on your own, but unless you've had professional instruction you are likely just ingraining bad habits. A good training course will teach you what to practice.

Shooters will often leave a course amazed at how much they didn't know when they arrived and that is a positive thing. They are now on their way, they've become a student of the gun.

Parting Thoughts

If you are truly serious about defending yourself with a firearm and carrying one on your person on a regular basis there are several steps you should take. Apply for your CCW Permit, purchase a quality firearm that you can rely upon, get some training and then practice often.

It's really not all that complex of a formula but I'm dismayed at how many folks stop after the first step. When all is said and done, it's your life to preserve or not. The choice is ultimately up to you. At very least you should make an informed decision.

POST-SHOOTING: THE AFTERMATH

Assuming you were mentally alert and physically prepared for the armed confrontation that forced its way into your life you will now have to deal with aftermath or the post-shooting trauma. First and foremost you need to have clarity of mind regarding the events. By clarity of mind I mean that in your own mind, in your heart of hearts, you need to be assured that the actions you took were appropriate for the situation and that, based upon the circumstances, you had no other choice.

The natural human tendency after any type of trauma, not just gunfights, but crashes, fires, or disasters is to replay the event over and over in your head. During these replays it is also natural to have doubts and critique your own actions. Remember this; only the living can enjoy the luxury of self-examination. If you survived the fight you did something right.

When you are running that mental replay keep in mind that your actions were based upon the information you had available at that moment in time, not the day after. In a deadly assault you will likely have mere seconds, if not fractions of seconds to act to save your life or that of someone else. Information discovered after the fact cannot have bearing over your initial actions.

Here is an example. A robber points a gun at you and threatens your life or that of your loved one. You respond in kind, draw and shoot the attacker. During the post-shooting investigation it is determined that your assailant had not loaded his gun. He could not have shot you with it if he had wanted to. A rational, moral person will be tempted to feel guilty. When replaying the event in your mind you might begin to doubt yourself. "Did I act too quickly? Should I have given him time to surrender?"

Do not allow this post-shooting information to cloud your mind. When that gun was pointed at you and the robber threatened to kill you all you knew at that moment in time was that a single bullet from a gun could end your life. That was the information you had to go on. Self-doubt and misplaced guilt can cause very real mental trauma. Be aware of this natural tendency and resist it.

Training and education are also key factors in surviving the post-shooting aftermath. Through proper training you will come to understand what actions are appropriate for given situations. Education in justifiable use of force and how the law relates to it will give you a solid mental foundation to know which actions are lawful and which are not.

You need to be proactive with your training and education. They both need to take place before you are required to use force for self-defense. Take the time now to consider your level of education and training regarding justifiable use of force. Like car insurance, you need to have it before the crash, not after.

CHAPTER 6

THE COACH AND INSTRUCTOR

HOW DO WE SERVE THE NEW SHOOTER?

For generations the tradition of firearms ownership was a family affair, fathers passed down their knowledge of guns and shooting to their sons. As our nation grew wives and daughters began taking to the field and learned to use firearms to defend the home. It was simply expected that every member of the American household would be able to safely and effectively use firearms.

Then came the modern, "enlightened" era. Men and women were deceived into believing that only their personal pleasure was important. Self-gratification was all that they needed to concern themselves. Matters such as protecting the family and home were best left to others. The government through, local police agencies, was now responsible for protecting the homestead, not the father and mother.

As members of our society abdicated their personal responsibilities, the generational chain began to break down. Sons were no longer taught by their fathers to use firearms. Brides demanded that their new husbands "get rid of" their guns and the "enlightened" husband acquiesced. These people were satisfied that at some future date they could always obtain guns if and when they wanted to.

New Modern Era

Today, rather they commuting to work in flying cars, living in underwater cities or taking vacations to the moon, fathers and mothers have lost their jobs and homes. Disposable income has shrunk and retirement plans shriveled. Natural and man-made disasters have brought mob violence and wide-spread looting directly to the front door step. The threat of terrorism nags at the mind of responsible citizens.

For those of us who never left the fold, we watch with quiet amazement every time there is a riot or disaster as the "enlightened" people flock to gun stores looking for the same barbaric tools they once eschewed. Historically, a post-disaster spike in firearm sales and interest in personal defense is over rather quickly.

When we consider the sales figures of personal defense firearms and ammunition over the last few years it seems that the situation is no longer a 'spike' but a genuine trend. I have many close friends who are firearms trainers and they all report that the number of new shooters, particularly women, attending their classes has risen dramatically.

Serving the new gun owner

Given the thousands upon thousands of new gun owners in the United States it only makes sense that we take a moment to consider how we, the faithful ones, can best help them or serve their needs. Let's break this discussion down into a few different categories beginning the firearms manufacturers.

Manufacturers

While those in the firearms industry are not perfect, for the last several years they have indeed been gearing new products toward the novice gun owner. Walking into a gun store to purchase your first firearm can be a pretty daunting task. There is so much from which to choose and gun people all speak their own language.

Smith&Wesson, Ruger, Glock, Springfield Armory, Kel-Tec, Kahr Arms, and SIG Sauer all come immediately to mind as they have introduced or re-introduced handguns that are uncomplicated and affordable. That is really what the novice shooter needs; a gun they can afford and operate without difficulty. Many of these manufacturers are offering complete pistol kits that come with a holster and magazine pouch.

When it comes to choosing ammunition, the task is again complicated by the fact that so many different styles of ammunition are available for each chambering. Many ammo makers, Federal, Winchester, Remington, and Hornady to name a few, have updated their packaging and specifically labeled the boxes as "Personal Defense" or "Home Defense".

Several firearms and ammunition manufacturers have hired big name professional trainers to do live instruction and YouTube videos in an effort to educate the public. Television shows such as Best Defense, Personal Defense TV, and Student of the Gun all reach out to new and experienced gun owners alike.

Husbands

Alright guys, suck it up because I'm talking to you. Let's say that for whatever reason your wife has decided that she wants to learn to shoot and she wants a gun. Great! Now stop yourself and realize this. You are the last person in the world that should be teaching your wife to shoot. Think about it. In your wife's eyes you are the man who forgets to buy milk, leaves the toilet seat up, and sniffs his T-shirts to see if they are still clean enough to wear. I truly believe that Albert Einstein's wife once said "Some genius you are, you can't even remember to put the trash out."

I have taught thousands of police officers, US Military troops and citizens young and old to use rifles, pistols and shotguns, but when my wife wanted to get her concealed carry permit I found someone else to train her. Do yourself a favor, keep the divorce lawyers out of the situation and find a reputable, professional trainer to teach your wife to shoot.

When it comes to what gun, specifically handgun, to buy for your wife, remember this; the gun is for HER.

Handing down your old pistol to your wife so you have an excuse to buy a new one is not cool. After your wife has some training and experience let her pick out her own gun. Buying a new gun and then taking training can be a waste of time and money. Borrowed or rented guns are a lot more cost effective. Too often folks will buy a brand new gun before they get training only to find out afterward that don't like how the gun feels or operates.

Along the same lines, your favorite gun is not necessarily going to be your wife's favorite. And, for the love of all that is holy, guys please stop buying your wives compact .40 caliber pistols. To your lovely wife it's like having a firecracker detonate in her hands with every shot. I would offer that a 9mm or .380 ACP pistol that a person enjoys shooting is a far better choice than a shaper recoiling gun that they only tolerate.

I recently had a husband / wife team show up for training with two brand new pistols; a GLOCK 22 for him and a GLOCK 23 for her. The small statured, inexperienced wife struggled for the entire live-fire portion of the class. She was literally being taught to flinch with every shot. Guys, park your machismo and stop handing your wives and girlfriends hard-kicking blasters. They'll gut it out and shoot the guns to please you but most won't enjoy the experience nor will they voluntarily do it again.

Range Gurus

We all know the range gurus, the guys who spent more time on the range talking than they do shooting. They love to regale you with tales of their favorite guns and opinions about the best this or that. That's all well and good, but new shooters don't need to hear your war stories and tall tales, they need encouragement.

The second most intimidating thing for novice gun owner to do after they've purchased a gun is to go to a public range and shoot it. Whether real or perceived they feel as though all eyes are upon them, judging them. Many novice shooters are driven away by arrogant or condescending range gurus. Don't be that guy. You were the new guy once yourself. Take a second to listen to the new shooter before you tell them what gear they should have instead. If their gun and gear doesn't work for them they'll figure it out.

Parting Thoughts

The good news is that we are slowly but surely moving back toward gun ownership being a common thing in American households. The anti-gun ninnies can keep screaming about how you are a thousand times more likely to be killed with your own gun than to stop a burglar but the American public in ever increasing numbers realizes the truth.

Every day novice shooters and new gun owners are entering the fold. What these folks need is for us to nurture their interest not overwhelm them with our opinions. The firearms industry is providing products for the new shooter and professional trainers are offering classes to help the novice. The last piece of the puzzle is you, the experienced gun guy. You are the neighbor, co-worker, husband, uncle, or friend that can make the difference and welcome the new shooter and gun owner to the fold.

BECOME A BETTER INSTRUCTOR: A SIMPLE THREE STEP PROGRAM

If you are truly passionate about a subject or field of endeavor, whatever this might be, it is natural to want to share your experience and knowledge with others. For active shooters, this desire often will first manifest itself through very informal training.

This situation normally begins with a simple question from a novice gun owner. I have heard this a hundred times, "You're a 'gun guy,' what do you think about…?" You give that person what you believe is a good answer and this many times satisfies them.

However, the genuinely sincere novice will frequently follow up with more specific questions. From a defensive handgun standpoint they will ask about what kind of holster to buy, what ammunition to use, what is the best way to hold the pistol, etc. It's not long before your casual conversation becomes an actual period of instruction.

Experienced shooters that are particularly serious about their passion can seek out training to become a certified instructor. The NRA is the largest private organization providing instructor training to individuals.

With your Instructor's Certificate in hand you are now ready teach others. You know all about firearms safety, range safety, sight picture and trigger squeeze. You can explain the difference between the isosceles and the Weaver and which one works best for you. Possessing knowledge, however, is only a part of being a good instructor, how to effectively impart that knowledge to others is the next step.

In my current position I am working as a full-time instructor teaching others about small arms and tactics. Even though I have been providing instruction for many years, a recent refresher gave me the inspiration to pen this section. My desire in the next couple of pages is to give you a brief overview of some of the traits and techniques that professional instructors all share. I have broken this down into a three-step format for easy digestion.

Step1: You

The first step can be both the easiest and most difficult of all. This portion is all about you as an instructor. The reason I say it can be the easiest is that you don't need someone else's blessing or approval. You have the power to be the best instructor you can be. However, if you have developed and ingrained a number of bad habits over the years, making changes can be difficult. You must have an open mind and be willing to seek self-improvement.

Good instructors should possess three basic traits; Knowledge, Ability, and Personality. Regarding knowledge, you need to be a subject matter expert in the field you are teaching. Yes, I know "expert" smacks of arrogance. What this really means is know your subject inside and out. You should have a depth of knowledge, much more that the basics. At the same time know your limitations and don't try to fake your way through a class. It might work once but eventually you will get tripped up.

Ability simply refers to your being able to lead a class and direct the course of instruction in a productive and effective manner. Some people have a natural ability to lead and others have to work at it but over time they will develop this trait. Standing in front of a classroom full of strangers, or friends for that matter, and leading them through a course of instruction takes some serious ability. Naturally, ability indicates that you can actually perform the tasks you are expecting your students to perform.

The third trait, personality, is one that you have complete control over. Under the personality heading you have your appearance, behavior and demeanor. Appearance is a big factor as humans naturally judge others by what they first see.

It doesn't matter how gee whiz cool your course is if you look like you slept in your clothes and your hair hasn't encountered a comb since your fourth grade school picture. Take a good, hard look in the mirror before you step in front of a class.

Continuing on with behavior or demeanor, patience is the top of the list. You must have and exhibit patience with students. Frustration will show on your face and in your tone of voice. Practicing patience is paramount to effective teaching.

Step 2: Learning

In order to be an effective and productive teacher or instructor you must understand the Principles of Learning. Most readers will have heard the term "mirror thinking." That is, the majority of people instinctively assume that everyone else thinks the same way they do. This carries over into teaching as most instructors, without consciously doing so, will gravitate toward teaching the way that they learn best. The problem with this is that not everyone thinks the same way that you do; not everyone learns the same way.

There are generally four accepted learning styles. I say "generally accepted" as a caveat. I have attended several professional instructor courses and had varied amounts of emphasis put on the learning principles. Many courses will use different verbiage to describe the stages.

With that said, these methods or principles include abstract, reflective, concrete, and active. Abstract learners take a more analytical approach, they learn best through lectures from subject matter experts. Reflective learners like to observe or reflect on the material. This group learns through lecture but also through films and reading on their own.

Concrete learners use actual materials. They learn by taking the pieces of the puzzle and assembling them. The concrete learner will have to do it themselves first before truly appreciating the lesson. This category includes those who rely heavily on their own personal experience and personal judgments.

Your active learners prefer to get involved and put their hands on. They learn best under lab exercises or with practical application. The trial and error way of learning appeals to them.

As you can see from Step 2, understanding how different people learn is vital to successfully teaching a group. Too many instructors are active learners so they will quickly gloss over the lecture or classroom portion. There may be students in your class who learn best through lecture and to do so would be cheating them. A good course will involve lecture, demonstration, and hands-on training.

Step 3: Communication

In the first two steps we have prepared ourselves, both mentally and physically, we know our material inside and out and we understand that different people with learn best in different ways. Now it is time to take that knowledge, that course material, and effectively deliver it to an eager class of students.

Put simply, communication is the effective transfer and reception of information from one person to another. Note that good communication is not a one way street. It is your responsibility to clearly and accurately deliver the information and also to ensure that what was said or demonstrated has been understood by the person or persons on the receiving end. If you can't do this it's like talking into a dead cell phone. You can talk all day long but no one on the other end is hearing you.

First off let's look as effectively delivering the message. In addition to knowing your material, you need to have your material organized and ready to present. Have your course outline organized in the manner you wish to deliver it. If you are using audio/visual materials such as PowerPoint, transparencies or DVD's/videos, check all of your material and ensure the machines are working *before* the students are sitting in front of you. Fumbling with a PowerPoint program or trying to figure out how an overhead projector works while students are watching does not inspire confidence and leads to frustration. Believe me, I have been there.

Speak clearly and emphasize important points. If your voice does not carry well consider using a microphone / amplifier set up. Don't yell at students, but be sure the folks in the last row can hear you without difficulty.

Along the same lines, if you are using a chalkboard or dry-erase whiteboard, write big enough and dark enough for those in the back row to see. Also, teach to the class not the board. Refrain from talking to the board with your back to the class. If you need to write on the board take a moment to do so then continue your lecture. A few short pauses in a class can be a good thing.

When it comes to ensuring that the message has been received, there are several ways to confirm this. Eye contact is an excellent way. You should be making eye contact with the class anyway. If your students are with you and comprehending the material you will see it in their eyes and by the expressions on their faces. If they all look like cows staring at an oncoming train you need to slow down and clarify the material.

Try not to wait until the end of class to ask for questions. Ask thought-provoking questions as well as factual questions throughout the course. An example of a thought- provoking question might be, "What types of handgun actions are available?" The students will take a moment to think of all the different types of actions. A factual question has only one correct answer, IE "What caliber was the original Colt M1911A1 pistol?"

Lastly, a written test or practical examination will determine just how effective the instructor was in communicating the course information. If half of the class fails the test, you might need to examine your teaching ability and go over your method of instruction. Subsequently, if all or the majority of the class successfully completes the test or exam you can be assured that you are communicating effectively.

Closing Thoughts

The old joke is, "Those who can't do, teach." While that may have once been true, a professional instructor can both do and teach. Also, as we have considered in the previous pages, it takes a lot more than the ability to do something to teach it.

It is also true that teaching is one of the truest ways to become a devoted student to that subject. From a personal point of view, I find that I learn something new or uncover a hidden truth from nearly every course I teach.

If you have the time, teach someone else about the shooting sports. You will introduce them to an activity they can enjoy for a life time.

GEARING UP FOR SUCCESS

The old saying goes, "Those who cannot do teach." While there may be some validity to that, when it comes to coaching others, some of the best coaches are those who have not only done it, but done it well. Consider professional sports leagues like the NFL and the NBA.

Many of the most successful coaches are those who excelled in the sport when they were younger.

When we are talking about the shooting sports whether it involves rifle, handgun, or shotgun, one of the greatest ways to give back to the sport you love is to be an instructor or coach for up and coming shooters. I know in the precision marksmanship game, the coach is an essential figure and factors heavily into the success of the individual.

Even the greatest athletes in the world have coaches. The coach is the one who catches those minute errors that you don't realize you are making. The coach encourages you and helps your "keep your head in the game." And, occasionally, the coach is the one who puts his foot in your backside to get you back on track.

Over twenty years ago I became a Rifle and Pistol Marksmanship Coach when I was in the U.S. Marines. I was honored to be chosen amongst a group of expert riflemen for this duty. The Marine Corps has understood for decades that in addition to the Primary Marksmanship Instructor, the coach is a necessary member of the team.

Though my active-duty career is long over, today I am working with the next generation of American servicemen and women to improve their marksmanship skills and in a roundabout way show them how to become coaches for their brothers in arms. While being a good coach is largely cerebral in nature, there is also a gear factor that can't be ignored. To be a good coach or instructor you should possess several pieces of equipment that will help you get your job done.

The Bag

Before we dive into our list of miscellaneous gear we probably should have something to carry it all around in. There are a number of companies out there making high quality packs Blackhawk, Blue Force Gear and Maxpedition are some of them.

This is a good time to mention proper hydration. Most backpack makers have hydration bladder to go along with their packs. Regardless of what container you carry your water in; the most important factor is to drink water at regular intervals throughout the day. Waiting until you feel thirsty is *not* the time to start drinking. If you feel thirsty you are already behind the power curve.

In addition to making sure you are properly hydrated, you need to ensure your shooter or shooters is/are drinking water regularly as well. Some shooters are so focused on precision that they neglect to drink water. Reminding them is part of being a good coach.

Comfort

Though a bad day at the range beats a good day at work; your days can be long and tiresome if you aren't prepared for them. Having a few thoughtful items in your pack will minimize the physical discomfort and help you focus on the important stuff.

In my pack I have both elbow and knee pads, again these particular ones came from BlackHawk. While I only use the elbow pads on occasion, when I do need them there is little substitute.

As for the knee pads, I constantly find myself kneeling down next to a shooter to offer advice and encourage them. I don't know about you, but I am too old not to protect my knees. If you are a young coach, start protecting your knees now. You will need them when you get older.

Another very useful and oft overlooked comfort item is a cotton scarf, bandana, or Shemaugh. The Tactical Shemaugh from the BlackHawk catalog comes in OD green or Coyote tan and is made of 100 percent cotton. The scarf is 44x44 inches and is great for wiping the sweat off your brow and face or covering the back of your neck to guard against sunburn. Of course, you can just spread it out on the ground to keep from losing those small parts and springs during cleaning or maintenance.

Eyes and Ears

Anyone that is involved in shooting sports needs eye and ear protection. If you are serious about the sport, you really need to invest in a set of electronically enhanced hearing protection.

If you are coaching or instructing someone it's always a plus to be able to hear them. Electronically enhanced hearing protection blocks out the bad noise and amplifies the good sounds. Like your knees, you will appreciate your hearing as you get older. Naturally, you will want to keep several sets of foamy, disposable ear plugs in your range bag for spectators, shooters who forgot theirs, and yourself.

Eye protection is another must have. For the last year or so I have been using the Sawfly™ and the Viper protective eyewear from Revision. The Sawfly set has dark tinted, yellow, and clear interchangeable lenses. Also, as I wear prescription glasses, Revision offers snap-in prescription lenses. The entire kit is contained in a padded hard case.

While on the subject of eyes and vision, no coach should be without a set of quality binoculars. Yes, spotting scopes are valuable, but a five pound spotting scope is not something you are going to carry every day in your pack.

Useful Gear

There are a number of other items a good coach should have in their pack; a cleaning kit with a range rod is one of them. I keep a Kleen-Bore kit with me. It has a multi-section cleaning rod, AP brush, lubricant and patches. The Peltor earmuffs and this cleaning kit can be had from the giant Brownell's catalog.

Speaking of which, I picked up a really neat accessory from Brownell's a while back. They are earmuff covers. Made from a soft cotton material, these muff-covers have an elastic band and fit over most any kind of protective muffs you can imagine. In the summer they keep the sweat off of your ears. In the winter they provide a barrier between your ears and the cold plastic muffs. Don't procrastinate, buy a set now.

When you are out on the range you never know what screw is going to come loose or what will break. As I would rather not carry a ten-pound tool box around with me, I put a SpydeRench multi-tool from Spyderco in my pack.

Many shooting competitions, especially long range precision matches, have specific times limits. Your shooter needs to focus on shooting, you as the coach need to watch the clock. This means you need a good watch, preferably one with a chronograph or a timer.

Miscellaneous

In the "other" column you are going to want to pack inexpensive but important items such as sunscreen and hand wipes. If you or your shooter has a sun-blistered neck, face or arms you aren't going to be able to focus on shooting. Also, range work is dirty work, spend a dollar or two and get a package of pre-moistened hand wipes to keep in your pack.

Clothing is too big a topic to cover completely in this piece but I will say this; invest in quality clothing and footwear. If you are uncomfortable you will not be effective as a coach.

If there is any chance of the range being wet or covered in heavy dew I would wear water-resistant boots. Cold, wet feet are not happy feet. BlackHawk has new waterproof boots lined with SympaTex™. They even have new cushioned boot socks to keep you feet happy.

Pick up a Gore-Tex™ rain jacket for those cool, wet mornings and afternoons. A fleece liner for that jacket will make you an even happier camper.

Closing Thoughts

If you have a love for shooting and can do it well, I would highly recommend that you get involved in instructing and coaching. Everyday new shooters get involved in the sport and they need dedicated individuals to mentor and motivate them. Coaching or instructing also has the effect of help you to become a better shooter or competitor. Working with others should be an inspiration to learn more and practice diligently.

While it is true that attitude, knowledge, and skill are the most important attributes for a coach. There is no getting around the fact that the right equipment can make you a more productive mentor on the range.

CLOSING THOUGHTS

Let me take a moment to thank you for your investment in this text. I am personally grateful to you for your patronage and belief in what it means to be a student of the gun. Let me leave you with just a few words of inspiration.

The path to greatness or mastery is never ending and, even though we realize this, we continue the journey. My advice to those on the path is to beware of the poisonous traps put out by the under-achiever who tells you it's not worth the effort and the enabler who tells you that you are already "good enough" so why try harder?

Every person moves down the path of greatness at their own pace. The key is to stay on the path and keep moving forward. When someone tells you that your journey is not worth the effort or that you can stop now because you are 'good enough' understand that they have already given up themselves. Resist the temptation to settle for 'C' student status. Achievement requires effort, dedication and sacrifice. Don't make the target bigger so it's easier to hit, make the target smaller and continue to improve.

Student of the Gun
A beginner once, a student for life.

ABOUT THE AUTHOR

PAUL G. MARKEL has worn many hats during his lifetime. He has been a U.S. Marine, Police Officer, Professional Bodyguard, and Small Arms and Tactics Instructor. Mr. Markel has been writing professionally for law enforcement and firearms periodicals for nearly twenty years with hundreds and hundreds of articles in print. Paul is a regular guest on nationally syndicated radio talk shows and subject matter expert on firearms training and use of force.

Mr. Markel has been teaching safe and effective firearms handling to students young and old for decades and has worked actively with the 4H Shooting Sports program over a decade. Paul holds numerous instructor certifications in multiple disciplines and has been employed as a Subject Matter Expert (SME) in the use of arms; nonetheless, he is and will remain a dedicated Student of the Gun.

CPSIA information can be obtained
at www.ICGtesting.com
Printed in the USA
BVHW080321141220
595600BV00008B/710